PENGUIN BOOKS

THE SURGEON OF CROWTHORNE

'A weird and wonderful story of an eccentric friendship, and a slice of history' *Sunday Times*

'What a revelation. Beautifully told and awe-inspiring' *Daily Mail*

'An extraordinary tale, and Simon Winchester could not have told it better ... a splendid book' *Economist*

'A vivid parable – full of suspense, pathos and humour' *Wall Street Journal*

'A cracking read' *Spectator*

'The linguistic detective story of the decade' *The New York Times*

'Masterful ... one of those rare stories that combine human drama and historical significance' *Independent*

Simon Winchester was born and educated in England, has lived in Africa, India and China, and now lives in the Berkshire Hills of western Massachusetts. Having reported from almost everywhere during more than thirty years as a foreign correspondent, he now contributes to a variety of American and British magazines and makes regular broadcasts for the BBC.

Simon Winchester's other books include *Outposts: Travels to the Remains of the British Empire*; *Korea: A Walk through the Land of Miracles*; *The Pacific*; *Pacific Nightmare*, a fictional account of the aftermath of the Hong Kong hand-over; *Prison Diary, Argentina*, the story of three months spent in a Patagonian jail on spying charges during the Falklands war; *The River at the Centre of the World – A Journey up the Yangtze, and Back in Chinese Time*; the number-one international bestseller *The Surgeon of Crowthorne*; and *The Map that Changed the World*, which tells the extraordinary story of William Smith, pioneering geologist of the British Isles. His most recent book is *Krakatoa: The Day the World Exploded*.

THE SURGEON
OF CROWTHORNE

A Tale of Murder, Madness
and the *Oxford English Dictionary*

SIMON WINCHESTER

PENGUIN BOOKS

PENGUIN BOOKS

Published by the Penguin Group
Penguin Books Ltd, 80 Strand, London WC2R 0RL, England
Penguin Putnam Inc., 375 Hudson Street, New York, New York 10014, USA
Penguin Books Australia Ltd, 250 Camberwell Road, Camberwell, Victoria 3124, Australia
Penguin Books Canada Ltd, 10 Alcorn Avenue, Toronto, Ontario, Canada M4V 3B2
Penguin Books India (P) Ltd, 11 Community Centre, Panchsheel Park, New Delhi – 110 017, India
Penguin Books (NZ) Ltd, Cnr Rosedale and Airborne Roads, Albany, Auckland, New Zealand
Penguin Books (South Africa) (Pty) Ltd, 24 Sturdee Avenue, Rosebank 2196, South Africa

Penguin Books Ltd, Registered Offices: 80 Strand, London WC2R 0RL, England

www.penguin.com

First published by Viking 1998
Published in Penguin Book 1999
46

Copyright © Simon Winchester, 1998
All rights reserved

Frontispiece: the 'Call to the Contributors' has been reproduced
from a *New English Dictionary* pamphlet of April 1879,
by permission of Oxford University Press

The moral right of the author has been asserted

Set in Monotype Bembo
Printed in England by Clays Ltd, St Ives plc

To the memory of

G. M.

Contents

AN APPEAL

TO THE

ENGLISH-SPEAKING AND ENGLISH-READING PUBLIC

TO READ BOOKS AND MAKE EXTRACTS FOR

THE PHILOLOGICAL SOCIETY'S

NEW ENGLISH DICTIONARY.

———

In November 1857, a paper was read before the Philological Society by Archbishop Trench, then Dean of Westminster, on 'Some Deficiencies in our English Dictionaries,' which led to a resolution on the part of the Society to prepare a Supplement to the existing Dictionaries supplying these deficiencies. A very little work on this basis sufficed to show that to do anything effectual, not a mere Dictionary-Supplement, but a new Dictionary worthy of the English Language and of the present state of Philological Science, was the object to be aimed at. Accordingly, in January 1859, the Society issued their 'Proposal for the publication of a New English Dictionary,' in which the characteristics of the proposed work were explained, and an appeal made to the English and American public to assist in collecting the raw materials for the work, these materials consisting of quotations illustrating the use of English words by all writers of all ages and in all senses, each quotation being made on a uniform plan on a half-sheet of notepaper, that they might in due course be arranged and classified alphabetically and by meanings. This Appeal met with a generous response: some hundreds of volunteers began to read books, make quotations, and send in their slips to 'sub-editors,' who volunteered each to take charge of a letter or part of one, and by whom the slips were in turn further arranged, classified, and to some extent used as the basis of definitions and skeleton schemes of the meanings of words in preparation for the Dictionary. The editorship of the work as a whole was undertaken by the late Mr. Herbert Coleridge, whose lamented death on the very threshold of his work

An extract from the call to the contributors to what would eventually become the *Oxford English Dictionary*.

Preface

---

mysterious (mɪˈstɪərɪəs), *a.* [f. L. *mystērium*
MYSTERY[1] + OUS. Cf. F. *mystérieux*.]
   1. Full of or fraught with mystery; wrapt in mystery;
hidden from human knowledge or understanding;
impossible or difficult to explain, solve, or discover;
of obscure origin, nature, or purpose.

Popular myth has it that one of the most remarkable conversations in modern literary history took place on a cool and misty late autumn afternoon in 1896, in the small village of Crowthorne in Berkshire.

One of the parties to the colloquy was the formidable Dr James Murray, the then editor of what was later to be called the *Oxford English Dictionary*. On the day in question he had travelled fifty miles by train from Oxford to meet an enigmatic figure named Dr W. C. Minor, who was among the most prolific of the thousands of volunteer contributors whose labours lay at the core of the Dictionary's creation.

For very nearly twenty years beforehand these two men had corresponded regularly about the finer points of English lexicography. But they had never met. Minor seemed never willing or able to leave his home at Crowthorne, never willing to come to Oxford. He was unable to offer any kind of explanation, or do more than offer his regrets.

Murray, who himself was rarely free from the burdens of his work at his Scriptorium in Oxford, had none the less long dearly wished to see and to thank his mysterious and intriguing helper.

And particularly so by the late 1890s, with the Dictionary now well on its way to being half completed: official honours were being showered down upon its creators, and Murray wanted to make sure that all of those involved – even men so apparently bashful as Minor – were recognized for the valuable work they had done. He decided he would pay a visit; and the myth that came to surround that visit goes something like this.

Once he had made up his mind to go, he telegraphed his intentions, adding that he would find it most convenient to take a train that arrived at Crowthorne Station – then actually known as Wellington College Station, since it served the famous boys' school sited in the village – just after two on a certain Wednesday in November. Minor sent a wire by return to say that he was indeed expected and would be made most welcome. On the journey from Oxford the weather was fine; the trains were on time; the auguries, in short, were good.

   At the railway station a polished landau and a liveried coachman were waiting, and with James Murray aboard they clip-clopped back through the lanes of rural Berkshire. After twenty minutes or so the carriage turned into a long drive lined with tall poplars, drawing up eventually outside a huge and rather forbidding red-brick mansion. A solemn servant showed the lexicographer upstairs, and into a book-lined study, where behind an immense mahogany desk stood a man of undoubted importance. Murray bowed gravely, and launched into the brief speech of greeting that he had so long rehearsed:

   'A very good afternoon to you, sir. I am Dr James Murray of the London Philological Society, and editor of the *New English Dictionary*. It is indeed an honour and a pleasure to at long last make your acquaintance – for you must be, kind sir, my most assiduous helpmeet, Dr W. C. Minor?'

   There was a brief pause, an air of momentary mutual embarrassment. A clock ticked loudly. There were muffled footsteps in the hall. A distant clank of keys. And then the man behind the desk cleared his throat, and he spoke.

'I regret, kind sir, that I am not. It is not at all as you suppose. I am in fact the Superintendent of the Broadmoor Asylum for the Criminally Insane. Dr Minor is most certainly here. But he is an inmate. He has been a patient here for more than twenty years. He is our longest-staying resident.'

The official government files relating to this case are secret, and they have been locked away for more than a century. But I have recently been allowed to see them. What follows is the strange, tragic and spiritually uplifting story that they reveal.

Chapter One

Saturday Night in Lambeth Marsh

murder ('mɜːdə(r)), *sb.* Forms: *α.* 1 morþor, -ur, 3–4 morþre, 3–4, 6 murthre, 4 myrþer, 4–6 mur- thir, morther, 5 *Sc.* murthour, murthyr, 5–6 mur- thur, 6 mwrther, *Sc.* morthour, 4–9 (now *dial.* and *Hist.* or *arch.*) **murther;** *β.* 3–5 **murdre,** 4–5 **moerdre,** 4–6 **mordre,** 5 **moordre,** 6 **murdur, mourdre,** 6– **murder.** [OE. *morðor* neut. (with pl. of masc. form *morþras*) = Goth. *maurþr* neut.:–O Teut. **murþro^m*:–pre-Teut. **mrtro-m,* f. root **mer-: mor-: mr-* to die, whence L. *morī* to die, *mors (morti-)* death, Gr. μορτός, βροτός mortal, Skr. *mr.* to die, *mará* masc., *mr.ti* fem., death, *márta* mortal, OSl. *mĭrĕti,* Lith. *mirti* to die, Welsh *marw,* Irish *marþ* dead.

The word has not been found in any Teut. lang. but Eng. and Gothic, but that it existed in continental WGer. is evident, as it is the source of OF. *murdre, murtre* (mod.F. *meurtre*) and of med.L. *mordrum, murdrum,* and OHG. had the derivative *murdren* MURDER *v.* All the Teut. langs. exc. Gothic possessed a synonymous word from the same root with different suffix: OE. *morð* neut., masc. (MURTH[1]), OS. *morð* neut., OFris. *morth, mord* neut., MDu. *mort, mord* neut. (Du *moord*), OHG. *mord* (MHG. *mort,* mod.G. *mord*), ON. *morð* neut.:–OTeut. **murþo-:*–pre-Teut. **mrto-.*

The change of original *ð* into *d* (contrary to the general tendency to change *d* into *ð* before syllabic *r*) was prob. due to the influence of the AF. *murdre, moerdre* and the Law Latin *murdrum.*]

1. a. The most heinous kind of criminal homicide; also, an instance of this. In *English* (also *Sc.* and *U.S.*) *Law,* defined as the unlawful killing of a human being with malice aforethought; often more explicitly *wilful murder.*

In OE. the word could be applied to any homicide that was strongly reprobated (it had also the senses 'great wickedness', 'deadly injury', 'torment'). More strictly, however, it denoted *secret* murder, which in Germanic antiquity was alone regarded as (in the modern sense) a crime, open homicide being considered a private wrong calling for blood-revenge or com- pensation. Even under Edward I, Britton explains the AF. *murdre* only as felonious homicide of which both the per- petrator and the victim are unidentified. The 'malice afore- thought' which enters into the legal definition of murder, does not (as now interpreted) admit of any summary definition. Until the Homicide Act of 1957, a person might even be guilty of 'wilful murder' without intending the death of the victim, as when death resulted from an unlawful act which the doer knew to be likely to cause the death of some one, or from injuries inflicted to facilitate the commission of certain offences. By this act, 'murder' was extended to include death resulting from an intention to cause grievous bodily harm. It is essential to 'murder' that the perpetrator be of sound mind, and (in England, though not in Scotland) that death should ensue within a year and a day after the act presumed to have caused it. In British law no degrees of guilt are recognized in murder; in the U.S. the law distinguishes 'murder in the first degree' (where there are no mitigating circumstances) and 'murder in the second degree' (though this distinction does not obtain in all States).

In Victorian London, even in a place as louche and notoriously crime-ridden as the Lambeth Marsh, the sound of gun-shots was a rare event indeed. The Marsh was a sinister place, a jumble of slums and sin that crouched, dark and ogre-like, on the bank of the Thames just across from Westminster; few respectable Londoners would ever admit to venturing there. It was a robustly violent part of town as well – the footpad lurked in Lambeth, there had once been an outbreak of garrotting, and in every crowded alley there were the roughest kinds of pickpocket. Fagin, Bill Sikes and Oliver Twist would have all seemed quite at home in Victorian Lambeth: this was Dickensian London writ large.

But it was not a place for men with guns. The armed criminal was a phenomenon little known in the Lambeth of Gladstone's day, and very little known in the entire metropolitan vastness of London. Guns were costly, cumbersome, difficult to use, hard to conceal. Then, as today, the use of a firearm in the commission of a crime was thought of as somehow a very un-British act – and as something to be written about and recorded as a rarity. 'Happily,' proclaimed a smug editorial in Lambeth's weekly newspaper, 'we in this country have no experience of the crime of "shooting down", so common in the United States.'

So when a brief fusillade of three revolver shots rang out shortly after two o'clock on the moonlit Saturday morning of 17 February

1872, the sound was unimagined, unprecedented and shocking. The three cracks – perhaps there were four – were loud, very loud, and they echoed through the cold and smokily damp night air. They were heard – and considering their rarity were just by chance instantly recognized – by a keen young police constable named Henry Tarrant, who was then attached to Southwark Constabulary's 'L' Division.

The clocks had only recently struck two, his notes said later; he was performing with routine languor the duties of the graveyard shift, walking slowly beneath the viaduct arches beside Waterloo Railway Station, rattling the locks of the shopkeepers and cursing the bone-numbing chill.

When he heard the shots, Tarrant blew his whistle to alert any colleagues who he hoped might be on patrol near by, and began to run. Within seconds he had raced through the warren of mean and slippery lanes that made up what in those days was called a village, and emerged into the wide riverside swath of Belvedere Road, from where he was certain the sounds had come.

Another policeman named Henry Burton, who had heard the piercing whistle, as had a third, William Ward, rushed to the scene. According to Burton's notes, he dashed towards the echoing sound and came across his colleague Tarrant, who was by then holding a man, as if arresting him. 'Quick!' cried Tarrant. 'Go to the road – a man has been shot!' Burton and Ward raced in the direction of Belvedere Road and within seconds found the unmoving body of a dying man. They fell to their knees, and onlookers noted they had their helmets and gloves cast off, and were hunched over the victim.

There was blood gushing on to the pavement – blood staining a spot that would for many months afterwards be described in London's more dramatically minded papers as the location of a Heinous Crime, a Terrible Event, an Atrocious Occurrence, a Vile Murder.

The Lambeth Tragedy, the papers eventually settled upon calling it – as if the simple existence of Lambeth itself was not something of a tragedy. Yet this was a most unusual event, even by the diminished standards of the Marsh dwellers. For though the place where the killing occurred had over the years been witness to many strange scenes, the kind eagerly chronicled in the penny dreadfuls, this particular drama was to trigger a chain of consequences that was quite without precedent. And while some aspects of this crime and its aftermath were to turn out to be sad and barely believable, not all of them, as this account will show, were to be wholly tragic. Far from it, indeed.

Even today Lambeth is a singularly unlovely part of the British capital, jammed anonymously between the great fan of roads and railway lines that take commuters in and out of the city centre from the southern counties. These days the Royal National Theatre and the South Bank Centre stand there, built on the site of the fairgrounds for an entertainment that was staged in 1951 to help cheer up the blitz-battered and war-weary Londoners. Otherwise it is a cheerless and characterless sort of place – rows of prison-like blocks that house the lesser of the government ministries, the headquarters of an international oil company around which winter winds whip bitterly, a few unmemorable pubs and newspaper shops, and the lowering presence of Waterloo Station – lately expanded with the terminal for the Channel Tunnel expresses – which exerts its dull magnetic pull over the neighbourhood.

The railway chiefs of old never bothered to build a grand station hotel at Waterloo – though they did build monster structures of great luxury at the other London stations, like Victoria and Paddington, and even St Pancras and King's Cross. For Lambeth has long been one of the nastier parts of London; until very recently, with the further development of the South Bank Centre, no one of any style and consequence has ever wanted to linger there, neither a passenger back in the days of the Victorian boat-trains, nor anyone for any reason at all today. It is slowly improving; but its reputation dogs it.

A hundred years ago it was positively vile. It was low and marshy and undrained, a swampy gyre of pathways where a sad little stream called the Neckinger seeped into the Thames. The land was jointly owned by the Archbishop of Canterbury and the Duke of Cornwall, landlords who, rich enough in their own right, never bothered to develop it in the manner of the great lords of London – Grosvenor, Bedford, Devonshire – who created the squares and mansions and terraces on the far side of the river.

So it was instead a place of warehouses and tenant shacks, and miserable rows of ill-built houses. There were blacking factories and soap-boilers, small firms of dyers and lime-burners, and tanning yards where the leather-workers used a substance for darkening skins that was known as 'pure' and that was gathered from the streets each night by the filthiest of the local indigents – 'pure' being a Victorian term for dog turds.

A sickly smell of yeast and hops lay over the town, wafting from the chimneys of the great Red Lion Brewery that stood on Belvedere Road, just north of the Hungerford Bridge. And this bridge was symbolic of what encompassed the entire Marsh: the railways, hefted high over the swamps, on viaducts on which the trains (including those of the London Necropolis Railway, built to take corpses to Woking) chuffed and snorted, and across which miles of wagons lurched and banged. Lambeth was widely regarded as one of the noisiest and most sulphurous parts of a capital that already had a grim reputation for din and dirt.

Lambeth Marsh was also, as it happened, just beyond the legal jurisdiction of both the cities of London and Westminster. It belonged administratively, at least until 1888, to the county of Surrey – meaning that the relatively strict laws that applied to the capital's citizens did not apply to anyone who ventured, via one of the new bridges like Waterloo, Blackfriars, Westminster or Hungerford, into the wen of Lambeth. The village thus became fast known as a site of revelry and abandon, a place where public houses and brothels and lewd theatres abounded, and where a man could find entertainment of all kinds – and disease of all varieties – for no more than a handful of pennies. To see a play that would not pass muster with the London censors, or to be able to drink absinthe into the small hours of the morning, or to buy the choicest of pornography newly smuggled from Paris, or to have a girl of any age and not be concerned that a Bow Street Runner, or her parents, might chase after you – you 'went Surreyside', as they said, to Lambeth.

But, as with most slums, its cheapness attracted respectable men to live and work in Lambeth too, and by all accounts George Merrett was one of them. He was a stoker at the Red Lion Brewery; he had been there for the previous eight years, employed all the time as one of the gang who kept the fires burning through the day and night, keeping the vats bubbling and the barley malting. He was thirty-four years old and he lived locally, at 24 Cornwall Cottages on the Cornwall Road.

George Merrett was, like so many young workers in Victorian London, an immigrant from the countryside, and so was his wife, Eliza. He came from a village in Wiltshire, she from Gloucester-shire. They had both been farm labourers, and, with no protection from unions, no solidarity with their fellows, had been paid a pittance to perform pointless tasks for pitiless masters. They had met at a farm show in the Cotswolds, and vowed to leave together for the immeasurable possibilities that were offered by London, now only two hours away on the new express train from Swindon. They moved first to north London, where their oldest child, Clare, was born in 1860; then they shifted into the city centre; and finally in 1867, the family having become too large, costly and manual work too scarce, they found themselves near the brewery site in the bustling wen of Lambeth.

The young couple's surroundings and lodgings were exactly as the illustrator Gustave Doré had drawn on one of his horrified expeditions from Paris: a dim world of bricks and soot and screeching iron, of huddled tenements, of tiny backyards with privy and clothes-boiler and washing-line, and everywhere an air of damp and gritty stench, and even a rough-hewn rollicking hugger-mugger devil-may-care and peculiarly London type of good cheer. Whether the Merretts missed the fields and the cider and the skylarks, or whether they imagined that ideal truly ever was the world they had left, we shall never know.

For by the winter of 1871 George and Eliza had, as was typical of the inhabitants of the dingier quarters of Victorian London, a very substantial family: six children, ranging from Clare at nearly twelve years old, to Freddy at twelve months. Mrs Merrett was about to be confined with her seventh pregnancy. They were a poor family, as were most in Lambeth: George Merrett brought home twenty-four shillings a week, a miserable sum even then. With rent payable to the Archbishop, and with food needed for the eight ever open mouths, theirs were straitened circumstances indeed.

On the Saturday morning, just before 2 a.m., Merrett was awakened by a neighbour tapping on his window, as prearranged. He rose from bed, and readied himself for the dawn shift. It was a bitter morning, and he dressed as warmly as he could afford: a threadbare greatcoat over the kind of smock-jacket that Victorians called a slop, a tattered grey shirt, corduroy trousers tied at the ankle with twine, heavy socks and black boots. The clothes were none too clean: but he was to heave coal for the next eight hours, and could not be bothered with appearance.

His wife recalled him striking a light before leaving home: her last sight of him was under one of the bright gas lamps with which Lambeth's streets had recently been outfitted. His breath was visible in the cold night air – or maybe he was just puffing on his pipe – and he walked purposefully down to the end of Cornwall Road before turning left into Upper Ground, and then down to its continuation, Belvedere Road. The night was clear and starlit and, once his footsteps had faded, soundless except for the clanking and puffing of the ever present railway engines.

Mrs Merrett had no reason to be concerned: she assumed, as she had for each of the twenty previous nights on which her husband had worked the dawn shift, that all would be well. George was simply making his way as usual towards the high walls and ornate gates of the great brewery where he worked, shovelling coal beneath the shadow of the great red lion – the brewer's symbol – that was one of London's better-known landmarks. There may have been little money in the job; but working at so famous an institution as the Red Lion Brewery, well, that was some reason for pride.

But that night George Merrett never reached his destination. As he passed the entrance to Tenison Street, between where the south side of the Lambeth Lead Works abuts on to the north wall of the brewery, there came a sudden cry. A man shouted at him, appeared to be chasing him, was yelling furiously. Merrett was frightened: this was something more than a mere footpad, a silent and menacing figure who lurked in the dark with a cosh and a mask. Merrett began to run in terror, slipping and sliding on the frost-slick cobbles. He looked back: the man was still there, still chasing after him, still shouting angrily. Then, quite incredibly, he stopped and raised a gun at him, took aim and fired.

The shot missed, whistling past and striking the brewery wall. George Merrett tried to run faster. He cried out for help. There was another shot. Perhaps another. And then a final shot that struck the unfortunate Merrett in the neck. He fell heavily on to the cobbled pavement, his face down, a pool of blood spreading around him.

Moments later came the running footfalls of Constable Burton, who found the man, lifted him, attempted to comfort him. The other policeman, William Ward, summoned a passing hansom cab up from the still busy thoroughfare of Waterloo Road. They picked up the wounded man gently from the ground and hoisted him into the vehicle and ordered the driver to take them as fast as possible to St Thomas's Hospital, 500 yards further south on Belvedere Road, across from the Archbishop's London palace. The horses did their best, their hoofs striking fire from the cobbles as they rushed the victim to the emergency entrance.

It was a fruitless journey. Doctors examined George Merrett, attempted to close the gaping wound in his neck. But his carotid artery had been severed, his spine snapped by two large-calibre bullets.

The man who had perpetrated this unprecedented crime was, within moments of committing it, in the firm custody of Constable Henry Tarrant. He was a tall, well-dressed man of what the policeman described as 'military appearance', with an erect bearing and a haughty air. He held a smoking revolver in his right hand. He made no attempt to run, but stood silently as the policeman approached.

'Who is it that has fired?' asked the constable.

'I did,' said the man, and held up the gun.

Tarrant snatched it from him. 'Whom did you fire at?' he asked.

The man pointed down Belvedere Road, and to the figure lying motionless beneath a street lamp, just outside the brewery store. He made the only droll remark that history records him as having made – but a remark that, as it happens, betrayed one of the driving weaknesses of his life.

'It was a man,' he said, with a tone of disdain. 'You do not suppose I would be so cowardly as *to shoot a woman*!'

By now two other policemen had arrived on the scene, as had other inquisitive locals – among them the Hungerford Bridge toll-collector, who at first had not dared go out 'for fear I would take a bullet', and a woman undressing in her room in Tenison Street – a street in which it was apparently far from uncommon for women to be undressing at all hours. Constable Tarrant, pointing towards the victim and ordering his two fellow policemen to see what they could do for him, and prevent a crowd from gathering, escorted the supposed – and unprotesting – murderer to the Tower Street Police Station.

On the way his prisoner became rather more voluble, though Tarrant describes him as cool and collected, and clearly not affected by drink. It had all been a terrible accident, he said; he had shot the wrong man, he insisted. He was after someone else, someone quite different. Someone had broken into his room; he was simply chasing him away, defending himself as anyone surely had a perfect right to do.

'Don't handle me!' he then said, when Tarrant put a hand on his shoulder. But he added, rather more gently, 'You have not searched me, you know.'

'I'll do that at the station,' replied the constable.

'How do you know I haven't got another gun, and might shoot you?'

The policeman, plodding and imperturbable, replied that if he did have another gun, perhaps he would be so kind as to keep it in his pocket, for the time being.

'But I do have a knife,' replied the prisoner.

'Keep that in your pocket also,' said the stolid peeler.

There turned out to be no other gun; but a search did turn up a long hunting knife in a leather sheath, strapped to the man's braces behind his back.

'A surgical instrument,' he explained. 'I don't always carry it with me.'

Tarrant, once he had completed the search, explained to the desk-sergeant what had happened on Belvedere Road a few moments before. The pair then set about formally interviewing the arrested man.

His name was William Chester Minor. He was thirty-seven years old, and, as the policemen suspected from his bearing, a former army officer. He was also a qualified surgeon. He had lived in London for less than a year and had taken rooms locally, living alone in a simple furnished upstairs room near by at 41 Tenison Street. He evidently had no financial need to live so economically, for he was in fact a man of very considerable means. He hinted that he had come to this lubricious quarter of town for reasons other than the simply monetary, though what those reasons were did not emerge in the early interrogations. By dawn he was taken off to the Horsemonger Lane Gaol, charged with murder.

But there was one additional complication. Minor, it turned out, came from New Haven, Connecticut. He had a commission in the United States Army. He was an American.

This put a wholly new complexion on the case. The American Legation had to be told: and so in the mid-morning, despite being a Saturday, the Foreign Office formally notified the United States Minister in London that one of their army surgeons had been arrested and was being held on a charge of murder. The shooting on Belvedere Road, Lambeth, already because of the rarity of a shooting a *cause célèbre*, had now become an international incident.

The British papers, always eager to vent editorial spleen on their transatlantic rivals, made hay with this particular aspect of the story.

'The light estimation in which human life is held by Americans,' sniffed the *South London Press*,

may be noted as one of the most significant points of difference between them and Englishmen, and this is a most shocking example of it brought to our own doors. The victim of a cruel mistake has left a wife near confinement, and six children, the eldest only twelve, to the mercy of the world. It is gratifying to be able to record that the benevolent are coming forward with alacrity to the succour of the widow and the fatherless, and it is most sincerely to be hoped that all who can spare even a trifle will do their best to help the victims of this dreadful tragedy. The American Vice-Consul-General has, in the most thoughtful manner, opened a subscription list, and issued an appeal to Americans now in London to do what they can to alleviate the misery which an act of their countryman's has entailed.

Scotland Yard detectives were soon put on to the case, so important had it suddenly become that justice was seen to be done on both sides of the Atlantic. Since Minor, silent in his prison cell, was offering no help except to say that he did not know the victim and had shot him in error, they began to investigate any possible motive. In doing so, they uncovered the beginning of the trail of a remarkable and tragic life.

William Chester Minor had come to Britain the previous autumn, because he was ill – suffering at least in part from an ailment that some papers said 'was occasioned by the looseness of his private life'. It was suggested by the lawyer later appointed to defend him that his motivation in coming to England was to quieten a mind that had become, as Victorian doctors were apt to say, 'inflamed'. It was said that he had suffered 'a lesion on the brain', and many causes were put forward as to why this had happened. He had, his lawyer said, been in an asylum in America, and had taken retirement from the army on the grounds of ill health. He had been described by those who met him as 'a gentleman of fine education and ability, but with eccentric and dissolute habits'.

He first settled at Radley's Hotel, in the West End, and from there travelled by train to the major cities of Europe. He had brought with him a letter from a friend at Yale University, recommending him to John Ruskin, the celebrated British artist and critic. The two men had met, once; and Minor had been encouraged to take his water-colouring equipment along with him on his travels, and paint as a form of relaxation.

As the police imagined, Minor had moved from the West End shortly after Christmas 1871 and settled in Lambeth – a highly dubious choice for a man like this unless, as he later admitted, it offered him easy access to easy women. The American authorities told Scotland Yard they already had records of his behaviour as an army officer: he had a long history of frequenting what were then beginning to be called the 'tenderloin districts' of the cities in which he had been posted – most notably New York, where he had been sent to Governors Island and from where, on his leave days, he had gone regularly to some of Manhattan's roughest bars and music-halls. He had, it was said, a prodigious sexual appetite. He had caught venereal disease at least once, and a medical examination conducted at Horsemonger Lane Gaol showed that he had a case of gonorrhoea even now. He had caught it, he said, from a local prostitute, and had tried to cure it by injecting white Rhine wine into his urethra – an amusingly inventive attempt at a remedy, and one that, not surprisingly, failed.

His room, however, betrayed none of this seamier side. The detectives found his heavy leather and brass-bound portmanteaus, a great deal of money – mainly French, in twenty *livre* notes, a gold watch and chain, some Eley's bullets for his gun, his surgeon's commission and his letter of appointment as a captain in the US Army. There was also the letter of introduction to Ruskin, as well as a large number of water-colours, evidently completed by Minor himself. They were said by everyone who saw them to be of the highest quality – views of London, largely, many from the hills above the Crystal Palace.

His landlady, Mrs Fisher, said that he had been a perfectly good tenant but odd. He used to go away for several days at a time and, on returning, rather ostentatiously left his hotel bills – the Charing Cross Hotel was one she remembered, the Crystal Palace another – lying around for all to see. He seemed, she said, a very anxious man. Often he demanded that the furniture in his room be moved. He seemed afraid that people might break in.

He had one particular worry, Mrs Fisher told the police: Minor was apparently *formidably afraid of the Irish*. He would ask interminably whether or not she had any Irish servants working in the house – and, if so, demand that they be sacked. Did she have Irish visitors, any other Irish lodgers? He was always to be kept informed – of a possibility that, in Lambeth (which had a large population

of casual Irish labourers, working on the legions of London construction sites), was in fact all too real.

Yet it was not until the murder trial, held in early April, that the
full extent of Minor's illness was to become starkly apparent.
Among the score of witnesses who appeared before the Lord Chief
Justice in the court at Kingston Assizes – for this was Surrey's
jurisdiction still, not London's – three of them told a stunned
courtroom what they knew of the sad captain.

The London police, for a start, admitted they were already
somewhat acquainted with him, and that some time before the
murder knew that they had a troubled man living in their midst.
A Scotland Yard detective named Williamson testified that Minor
had come to the Yard three months before, complaining that men
were coming to his room at night, trying to poison him. He
thought that they were Fenians, members of the Irish Republican
Brotherhood, militant Irishmen, and they were bent on breaking
into his lodgings, hiding in the roof rafters, slipping through the
windows.

He made such allegations several times, said Williamson; shortly
before Christmas Minor had persuaded the Commissioner of Police
in New Haven to write a letter to the Yard, underlining the fears
that Minor felt. Even after the doctor moved to Tenison Street,
he kept in touch with Williamson: on 12 January he wrote that
he had been drugged, and was afraid that the Fenians were planning
to murder him and make it look as though his death were suicide.

A classic cry for help, one might think today. But an exasperated
Superintendent Williamson did nothing and told no one, beyond
noting with some contempt in his log-book that Minor was clearly
– and this was the first use of the word to describe the hapless
American – *insane*.

Then came a witness who had something very curious to offer
from his observations of Minor during the time the American was
held in remand in the cells at Horsemonger Lane.

The witness, whose name was William Dennis, was a member of a profession that has long since receded from modern memory: he was what was called a Bethlem Watcher. Usually he was employed at the Bethlehem Hospital for the Insane – such a dreadful place that the name has given us the word *bedlam* today – where his duties included watching the prisoner-patients through the night, to make sure that they behaved themselves and did not cheat justice by committing suicide. He had been seconded to the Horsemonger Lane Gaol in mid-February, he said, to watch the nocturnal activities of the strange visitor. He had watched him, he testified, for twenty-four nights.

It was a most curious and disturbing experience, Mr Dennis told the jury. Each morning Minor would wake and immediately accuse him of having taken money from someone, in order specifically to molest him while he slept. Then he would spit, dozens of times, as though trying to remove something that had been put into his mouth. He would next leap from his bed and scrabble about underneath, looking for people who, he insisted, had hidden there and were planning to annoy him. Dennis told his superior, the prison surgeon, that he was quite certain Minor was mad.

From the police interrogation notes came the evidence of an imagined motive for the crime – and with them a further indication of Minor's patent instability. Each night, Minor had told his questioners, unknown men – often lower class, often Irish – would come to his room while he was sleeping. They would maltreat him, they would violate him in ways he could not possibly describe. For months, ever since these nocturnal visitors had begun to torment him, he had taken to sleeping with his Colt service revolver, loaded with five cartridges, beneath his pillow.

On the night in question he awoke with a start, certain that a man was standing in the shadows at the foot of his bed. He reached under the pillow for his gun: the man saw him and took to his heels, running down the stairs and out of the house. Minor followed him as fast as he could, saw a man running down into Belvedere

Road, was certain that this was the intruder, shouted at him, then fired four times, until he had hit him and the man lay still, unable to harm him further.

The court listened in silence. The landlady shook her head. No one could get into her house at night without a key, she said. Everyone slept very lightly. There could be no intruder.

And as final confirmation, the court then heard from the prisoner's stepbrother, George Minor. It had been a nightmare, said George, having brother William staying in the family house in New Haven. Every morning he would accuse people of trying to break into his room the night before and try to molest him. He was being persecuted. Evil men were trying to insert metallic biscuits, coated with poison, into his mouth. They were in league with others who hid in the attic, and came down at night while he was asleep, and treated him foully. Everything was punishment, he said, for an act he had been forced to commit while in the US Army. Only by going to Europe, he said, could he escape from his demons. He would travel, and paint, and live the life of a respected gentleman of art and culture – and the persecutors might melt away into the night.

The court listened in melancholy silence, while Minor sat in the dock, morose, shamed. The lawyer whom the American Consul-General had procured for him said only that it was clear that his client was insane, and that the jury should treat him as such.

The Chief Justice nodded his agreement. It had been a brief but sorry case, the defendant an educated and cultured man, a foreigner and a patriot, a figure quite unlike those wretches who more customarily stood in the dock before him. But the law had to be applied with just precision, whatever the condition or estate of the defendant; and the decision in this affair was in a sense a foregone conclusion.

For thirty years the law in such cases had been guided by what were known as the McNaghten Rules – named for the man who, in 1843, shot dead the private secretary to Sir Robert Peel, and who was acquitted on the grounds that he was so mad he could not tell right from wrong. The Rules, which judged criminal responsibility rather than guilt, were to be applied in this case, he told the jury. If they were convinced that the prisoner was 'of unsound mind' and had killed George Merrett while under some delusion of the kind that they had just heard about, then they must do as juries were wont to do in this extraordinarily lenient time in British justice: they were to find William Chester Minor not guilty on grounds of insanity, and leave the judge to make such custodial sanction as he felt prudent and necessary.

And this is what the jury did, without deliberation, late on the afternoon of 6 April 1872. They found Minor legally innocent of a murder that everyone including him knew he had committed. The Lord Chief Justice then applied the only sentence that was available to him – a sentence still passed occasionally today, and that has a beguiling charm to its language, despite the swingeing awfulness of its connotations.

'You will be detained in safe custody, Dr Minor,' said the judge, 'until Her Majesty's Pleasure be known.' It was a decision that was to have unimaginable and wholly unanticipated implications, effects that echo and ripple through the English literary world to this day.

The Home Department (more familiarly the Home Office) took brief note of the sentence, and made the further decision that Minor's detention – which, considering the severity of his illness, was likely to occupy the rest of his natural life – would have to be suffered in the newly built showpiece of the British penal system, a sprawling set of red-brick blocks located behind high walls and spiked fences in the village of Crowthorne, in the royal county of Berkshire. Minor was to be transported as soon as was convenient from his temporary prison in Surrey to the Asylum for the Criminally Insane, Broadmoor.

Dr William C. Minor, Assistant Surgeon, United States Army,

now a forlornly proud figure from one of the oldest and best-regarded families of New England, was thus to be henceforward formally designated in Britain by Broadmoor Patient Number 742, and to be held in permanent custody as a Certified Criminal Lunatic.

Chapter Two

The Man Who Taught Latin to Cattle

polymath ('pɒlɪmæθ), *sb.* (*a.*) Also 7 **polumathe**. [ad. Gr. πολυμαθής having learnt much, f. πολυ- much + μαθ-, stem of μανθάνειν to learn. So F. *polymathe*.] **a.** A person of much or varied learning; one acquainted with various subjects of study.

1621 BURTON *Anat. Mel.* Democr. to Rdr. (1676) 4/2 To be thought and held Polumathes and Polyhistors. *a* **1840** MOORE *Devil among Schol.* 7 The Polymaths and Polyhistors, Polyglots and all their sisters. **1855** M. PATTISON *Ess.* I. 290 He belongs to the class which German writers ... have denominated 'Polymaths'. **1897** O. SMEATON *Smollett* ii. 30 One of the last of the mighty Scots polymaths.

---

philology (fɪ'lɒlədʒɪ). [In Chaucer, ad. L. *philologia*; in 17th c. prob. a. F. *philologie*, ad. L. *philologia*, a. Gr. φιλολογία, abstr. sb. from φιλόλογος fond of speech, talkative; fond of discussion or argument; studious of words; fond of learning and literature, literary; f. φιλο- PHILO- + λόγος word, speech, etc.]

1. Love of learning and literature; the study of literature, in a wide sense, including grammar, literary criticism and interpretation, the relation of literature and written records to history, etc.; literary or classical scholarship; polite learning.

It took more than seventy years to create the twelve tombstone-sized volumes that made up the first edition of what was to become the great *Oxford English Dictionary*. This heroic, royally dedicated literary masterpiece was on its completion in 1928 first called the *New English Dictionary*; but, with the publication of the first supplement in 1933, it became the *Oxford* ditto, and thenceforward was known familiarly by its initials, as the *OED*. Over the years following there were five supplements and then, half a century later, a second edition that integrated the first and all subsequent supplement volumes into one new twenty-volume whole. The book remains, in all senses, a truly monumental work – and with very little serious argument is still regarded as a paragon, the definitive guide to the language that, for good or ill, has now become the lingua franca of the civilized modern world.

Just as English is a very large and complex language, so the *OED* is a very large and complex book. It defines well over half a million words. It contains scores of millions of characters, and, in at least its early versions, many miles of handset type. The enormous and enormously heavy volumes of the second edition are bound in dark blue cloth: printers and designers and bookbinders worldwide see it as the apotheosis of their art, a handsome and elegant creation that looks and feels more than amply suited to its lexical thoroughness and accuracy.

The *OED*'s guiding principle, the principle that has set it apart from most other dictionaries, is its rigorous dependence on gathering *quotations* from the published or otherwise recorded use of English, and employing them to illustrate the sense of every single word in the language. The reason behind this unusual and tremendously labour-intensive style of editing and compiling was both bold and simple: by gathering and publishing selected quotations, the Dictionary could demonstrate the full range of characteristics of each and every word with a very great degree of precision. Quotations could show exactly how a word has been employed over the centuries, how it has undergone subtle changes of shades of meaning, or spelling, or pronunciation, and, perhaps most important of all, how and more exactly *when* each word was slipped into the language in the first place. No other means of dictionary compilation could do such a thing: only by finding and showing examples could the full range of a word's past possibilities be explored.

The aims of those who began the project, back in the 1850s, were bold and laudable, but there were distinct commercial disadvantages to their methods: it took an immense amount of time to construct a dictionary on this basis, it was too time-consuming to keep up with the evolution of the language it sought to catalogue, the work that finally resulted was uncommonly vast and needed to be kept updated with almost equally vast additions. It remains to this day for all of these reasons a hugely expensive book both to produce and to buy.

Yet withal it is widely accepted that the *OED* has a value far beyond its price; it remains in print and continues to sell well. It is the unrivalled corner-stone of any good library, an essential work for any reference collection. And it is still cited as a matter of course – 'the *OED* says . . .' – in parliaments and courtrooms and schools and lecture halls in every corner of the English-speaking world, and probably in countless others beyond.

It wears its status with a magisterial self-assurance, not least by giving its half million definitions a robustly Victorian certitude of tone. Some call the language of the Dictionary outdated, high-flown, even arrogant. Note well, they say by way of example, how infuriatingly prissy the compilers remain, when dealing with so modest an oath as *bloody*. The modern editors place the original *NED* definition between quotation marks – it is a word 'now constantly in the mouths of the lowest classes, but by respectable people considered "a horrid word", on a par with obscene or profane language, and usually printed in the newspapers (in police reports, etc.) "b—y"' – but even the modern definition is too lamely self-regarding for most: 'There is no ground for the notion,' today's entry reassures us, 'that "bloody", offensive as from associations it now is to ears polite, contains any profane allusion.'

It is those with ears polite, one supposes, who see in the Dictionary something quite different: they worship it as a last bastion of cultured Englishness, a final echo of value from the greatest of all modern empires. But even they will admit of a number of amusing eccentricities about the book, both in its selections and in the editors' choice of spellings; a small but veritable academic industry has recently developed, in which modern scholars grumble about what they see as the sexism and racism of the work, its fussily and outdated imperial attitude. (And to Oxford's undying shame there is even one word – though only one – that all admit was actually *lost* during the decades of its preparation – though the word was added in a supplement, five years after the first edition appeared.)

There are many such critics, and with the book being such a large and immobile target there will no doubt be many more. And yet most of those who come to use it, no matter how doctrinally critical they may be of its shortcomings, seem duly and inevitably to come, in the end, to admire it as a work of literature, as well as to marvel at its lexicographical scholarship. It inspires real and lasting affection: it is an awe-inspiring work, the most important book of reference ever made, and, given the unending importance of the English language, probably the most important that is ever likely to be.

The story that follows can fairly be said to have *two protagonists*. One of them is Minor, the murdering soldier from America; and there is one other. To say that a story has two protagonists, or three, or ten, is a perfectly acceptable, unremarkable modern form of speech. It happens, however, that a furious lexicographical controversy once raged over the use of the word – a dispute that helps to illustrate the singular and peculiar way that the *Oxford English Dictionary* has been constructed and how, when it flexes its muscles, it has a witheringly intimidating authority.

The word *protagonist* itself – when used in its general sense of meaning 'the chief personage' in the plot of a story, or in a competition, or as the champion of some cause – is a common enough word. It is, as might be expected of a familiar word, defined fully and properly in the Dictionary's first edition of 1928.

The entry begins with the customary headings that show its spelling, its pronunciation and its etymology (it comes from the Greek πρῶτος, meaning 'first', and ἀγωνιστής, meaning 'one who contends for a prize, a combatant, an actor', the whole meaning the leading character to appear in a drama). Following this comes the distinguishing additional feature of the *OED* – the editors' selection of a string of six supporting quotations – which is about the average number for any one *OED* word, though some merit many more. The editors have divided the quotations under two headings.

The first heading, with three sources quoted, shows how the word has been used to mean, literally, 'the chief personage in a drama'; the next three quotations demonstrate a subtle difference, in which the word means 'the leading personage in any contest', or 'a prominent supporter or champion of any cause'. By general consent this second meaning is the more modern; the first is the older and now somewhat archaic version.

The oldest quotation ever used to illustrate the first of these two meanings was that tracked down by the Dictionary's lexical detectives from the writings of John Dryden in 1671. ' 'Tis charg'd upon me,' the quotation reads, 'that I make debauch'd Persons . . . my protagonists, or the chief persons of the drama.'

This, from a lexicographical point of view, seems to be the English word's mother-lode, a fair clue that the word may well have been introduced into the written language in that year, and possibly not before. (But the *OED* offers no guarantee. German scholars in particular are constantly deriving much pleasure from winning an informal lexicographic contest that aims at antedating *OED* quotations: at the last count the Germans alone had found 35,000 instances in which the *OED* quotation was *not* the first; others, less stridently, chalk up their own small triumphs of lexical sleuthing, all of which Oxford's editors accept with disdainful equanimity, professing neither infallibility nor monopoly.)

This single quotation for *protagonist* is peculiarly neat, moreover, in that Dryden explicitly states the newly minted word's meaning within the sentence. So from the Dictionary editors' point of view there is a double benefit, of having the word's origin dated and its meaning explained, and both by a single English author.

Finding and publishing quotations of usage is an imperfect way of making pronouncements about origins and meanings, of course – but to nineteenth-century lexicographers it was the best way that had yet been devised, and it is a method that has not yet been bettered. From time to time experts succeed in challenging specific findings like this, and on occasions the Dictionary is forced to recant, is obliged to accept a new and earlier quotation, and to give to a particular word a longer history than the Oxford editors first thought. Happily *protagonist* itself has not so far been successfully challenged on grounds of its chronology. So far as the *OED* is concerned, 1671 still stands: the word has for 300 odd years been a member of that giant corpus known as the English vocabulary.

The word appears again, and with a new supporting quotation, in the 1933 supplement – a volume that had to be added because of the sheer weight of new words and new evidence of new meanings that had accumulated during the decades when the original Dictionary was being compiled. By now another shade of meaning had been found for it – that of 'a leading player at some game or sport'. A sentence supporting this, from a 1908 issue of *The Complete Lawn Tennis Player*, is produced in evidence.

But then comes the controversy. The other great book on the English language, Henry Fowler's hugely popular *Modern English Usage*, first published in 1926, insisted – contrary to what Dryden had been quoted as saying in the *OED* – that *protagonist* is a word that can only ever be used *in the singular*.

Any use suggesting the contrary would be grammatically utterly wrong. And not just wrong, Fowler declares, but *absurd*. It would be nonsense to suggest that there could ever be two characters in a play, both of whom could be described as *the most important*. One either is the most important person, or one is not.

It took more than half a century before the *OED* decided to settle the matter. The 1981 supplement, in the classically magisterial way of the Dictionary, tries to calm the excitable (and now, as it happens, late) Mr Fowler. It offers a new quotation, reinforcing the view that the word can be used plurally or singularly as the need arises. George Bernard Shaw, it says, wrote in 1950 that 'living actors have to learn that they too must be invisible while the *protagonists* are conversing, and therefore must not move a muscle nor change their expression'. Perhaps Fowler's great linguistic authority was technically correct but, the Dictionary explains in an expanded version of its 1928 definition, perhaps only in the specific terms of Greek theatre, for which the word was first devised.

In the common-sense world of modern English – the world which, after all, the great Dictionary was designed to fix and define – it is surely quite reasonable to have two or more leading players in any story. Many dramas have room for more than one hero, and both or all may be equally heroic. If the Ancient Greeks were one-hero dramatists, then so be it. In the rest of the world, there could be as many as the dramatists cared to write parts for.

Now there is a twenty-volume second edition of the *OED*, with all the material from the supplements fully integrated with the original work, and new words and forms that have emerged in the years since inserted as needs be. In that edition *protagonist* appears in what is currently considered to be its true fixity: with three main meanings, and nineteen supporting quotations. Dryden's remains unaltered, the first appearance of the word, *and* in the plural; and to give even greater weight to the notion that plural is a perfectly acceptable form, both *The Times* and the thriller-writer and medievalist Dorothy L. Sayers are quoted, in addition to Shaw. The word is thus now properly lexically set for all time, and is stated by the almost unchallengeable authority of the *OED* to be available for use in either the singular or the multiple.

Which happens to be just as well, considering, and to reiterate the point, the existence of two protagonists in this story.

The first one, as is already clear, is Dr William Chester Minor, the admitted and insane American murderer. The other is a man whose lifetime was more or less coincident with Minor's, although it was different in almost all its other aspects: he was named James Augustus Henry Murray. The lives of the two men were over the years to become inextricably and most curiously entwined.

And, moreover, both were to be entwined with the *OED*, since James Murray was to become for the last forty years of his life its greatest and most justly famous editor.

James Murray was born in February 1837, the eldest son of a tailor and linen-draper in Hawick, a pretty little market town in the valley of the River Teviot, in the Scottish borderlands. And that was about all that he really wished the world to know about himself. 'I am a nobody,' he would write towards the end of the century, when fame had begun to creep up on him. 'Treat me as a solar myth, or an echo, or an irrational quantity, or ignore me altogether.'

But it has long since proved impossible to ignore him, as he was to become a towering figure in British scholarship. Honours were showered on him during his lifetime, and he has achieved the standing of a mythic hero since his death. Murray's childhood alone, which was unmasked twenty years ago by his granddaughter Elisabeth, who opened his trunk of papers, hints temptingly that he was destined – despite his unpromising, unmonied, unsophisticated beginnings – for extraordinary things.

He was a precocious, very serious little boy; he turned steadily into an astonishingly learned teenager, tall, well built, with long hair and an early bright-red beard that added to his grave and forbidding appearance. 'Knowledge is power,' he declared on the flyleaf of his school exercise book, and added – for as well as having a working knowledge by the time he was fifteen of French, Italian, German and Greek, he, like all educated children then, knew Latin – '*Nihil est melius quam vita diligentissima.*'

He had a voracious appetite, an impassioned thirst, for all kinds of learning. He taught himself about the local geology and botany, he found a globe from which he could learn geography and foster a love for maps, he unearthed scores of textbooks from which he could take on the enormous burden of history; he observed and took pains to remember all the natural phenomena about him. His younger brothers would tell how he once awakened them late one night to show them the rising of the dog-star Sirius, whose orbit and appearance over the horizon he had calculated and that proved, to the family's sleepy exultation, to be perfectly correct.

He particularly cherished encountering and interrogating people he met who proved to be living links with history: he once found an ancient who had known someone present at the proclamation of William and Mary in 1689; then again, his mother would recount over and over how she had heard tell of the victory at Waterloo; and when he had children himself he would allow them to be dandled on the knees of an elderly naval officer who was present when Napoleon agreed to surrender.

He left school at fourteen, as did most of the poorer children of the British Isles. There was no money for him to go on to the fee-paying grammar school in nearby Melrose, and in any case his parents enjoyed some confidence in the lad's ability to teach himself – by pursuing, as he had vowed, the *vita diligentissima*. Their hopes proved well founded: James continued to amass more and more knowledge, if only (as he would admit) for the sake of knowledge itself, and often in the most eccentric of ways.

He engaged in furious digs at a multitude of archaeological sites all over the borderlands (which, being close to Hadrian's Wall, was a treasure-trove of buried antiquities); he made attempts to teach the local cows to respond to calls in Latin; he would read out loud, by the light of a minute oil lamp, the works of a Frenchman with the grand name of Théodore Agrippa d'Aubigné, and translate for his family, who gathered about him, fascinated.

He once tried to invent water-wings from bundles of pond iris, tied them to his arms but was turned upside-down by more buoyancy than he had calculated, and would have drowned (he was a non-swimmer) had not his friends rescued him by pulling him from the lake with his five-foot-long bow-tie. He memorized hundreds of phrases in Romany, the language of the passing gypsies; he learned bookbinding; he taught himself to embellish his own writings with elegant little drawings and flourishes and curlicues, rather like the monkish illuminators of the Middle Ages.

By seventeen this 'argumentative, earnest, naïve' young Scot was employed in his home town as an assistant head schoolmaster, eagerly passing on the knowledge that he had so keenly gained; by twenty he was a fully fledged headmaster of the local Subscription Academy; and with his brother Alexander he became a leading member of that most Victorian and Scottish of bodies, the local Mutual Improvement Institute. He gave his first lecture, 'Reading, Its Pleasures and Advantages', and went on to present learned papers to the local Literary and Philosophical Society on his new passions of phonetics, on the origins of pronunciations, on the foundations of the Scottish tongue, and, once he had discovered its delights, on the magic of Anglo-Saxon.

And yet all of this early promise seemed suddenly doomed, first by the onset of love and then by the upset of tragedy. For in 1861, when he was just twenty-four, Murray met and the following year married a handsome but delicate infant-school music teacher named Maggie Scott. Their wedding picture shows Murray a strangely tall, vaguely simian figure in his ill-fitting frock coat and baggy trews, a man with hugely long knee-brushing arms, an unkempt beard, hair already thinning by the peak, eyes narrow and intense; neither happy nor unhappy but full of thought, his mind seemingly filled with a kind of distracted foreboding.

Two years later they had a baby girl whom they christened Anna. But, as was wretchedly commonplace at the time, she died in infancy. Maggie Murray herself then fell gravely ill with consumption and was said by the Hawick doctors to be unlikely to withstand the rigours of another long Scottish winter. The recommended treatment was to sojourn in the South of France but that, given Murray's tiny schoolmaster's wage, was quite out of the question.

Instead the forlorn couple took off for London, and modest lodgings in Peckham. Murray, now twenty-seven, had to his bitter disappointment been forced by his domestic circumstances to abandon all of his current intellectual pursuits, all of his digging and delving and pronouncements on linguistics and on phonetics and the origins of words – on which topic he was then enjoying a lively correspondence with the notable scholar Alexander Melville Bell, father of the infinitely more famous Alexander Graham Bell. Economic necessity and marital duty – though he was devoted to Maggie, and never complained – had pressed him to become instead, and with a dreary predictability, a clerk in a London bank. With his employment, in starched cuffs, green eye-shade and a high stool at the back of the head office of the Chartered Bank of India, it seemed as though the story might have come to an ignominious end.

Not so. Within just a matter of months he was back in the traces. He had renewed his eccentric pursuit of learning – studying Hindustani and Achaemenian on his daily commute, trying to determine by their accents from which region of Scotland various London policemen came, lecturing on 'The Body and Its Architecture' before the Camberwell Congregational Church (where, as a confirmed and lifelong teetotaller, he was a keen member of their Temperance League), and even noting with amused detachment, while his sickly and well-loved Maggie was dying, that in her nightly delirium she lapsed into the broad Scots dialect of her childhood, and abandoned the more refined tones of a school-teacher. That small discovery, that marginal addition to his learning, went some way to helping him through the misery of her subsequent death.

And one would be right in wondering about this detachment: a year after her death Murray was engaged to another young woman and, a year later still, married. While he had clearly loved and admired Maggie Scott, it was soon abundantly clear that here in Ada Ruthven, whose father worked for the Great Indian Peninsular Railway and was an admirer of Humboldt, and whose mother claimed to have been to school with Charlotte Brontë, was a woman who was far more his social and intellectual equal. They were to remain devoted and to have eleven children together, ten of whom bore the middle name Ruthven, according to the wishes of the father-in-law.

A letter that Murray then wrote in 1867, his thirtieth year, applying for a post with the British Museum, offers some of the flavour of his barely believable range of knowledge (as well as his unabashed candour in telling people about it).

I have to state that Philology, both Comparative and special, has been my favourite pursuit during the whole of my life, and that I possess a general acquaintance with the languages & literature of the Aryan and Syro-Arabic classes – not indeed to say that I am familiar with all or nearly all of these, but that I possess that general lexical and structural knowledge which makes the intimate knowledge only a matter of a little application. With several I have a more intimate acquaintance as with the Romance tongues, Italian, French, Catalan, Spanish, Latin & in a less degree Portuguese, Vaudois, Provençal and various dialects. In the Teutonic branch, I am tolerably familiar with Dutch (having at my place of business correspondence to read in Dutch, German, French & occasionally other languages), Flemish, German, Danish. In Anglo-Saxon and Moeso-Gothic my studies have been much closer, I having prepared some works for publication upon these languages. I know a little of the Celtic, and am at present engaged with the Sclavonic, having obtained a useful knowledge of the Russian. In the Persian, Achaemenian Cuneiform, & Sanscrit branches, I know for the purposes of Comparative Philology. I have sufficient knowledge of Hebrew and Syriac to read at sight the Old Testament and Peshito; to a less degree I know Aramaic Arabic, Coptic and Phoenician to the point where it is left by Genesius.

It somewhat beggars belief that the Museum turned down his job application. Murray was initially crushed but soon recovered.

Before long he was consoling himself in a characteristic way – by comparing, in lexical terms, the sheep-counting numerology of the Wowenoc Indians of Maine with that of the moorland farmers of Yorkshire.

Murray's interest in philology might have remained that of an enthusiastic amateur, were it not for his friendship with two men. One was a Trinity College, Cambridge, mathematician named Alexander Ellis, and the other a notoriously pig-headed, colossally rude phonetician named Henry Sweet – the figure on whom Bernard Shaw would later base his character Professor Henry Higgins in *Pygmalion*, which was transmuted later into the eternally popular *My Fair Lady* (where Higgins was played, in the film, by the similarly rude and pig-headed actor Rex Harrison).

These men swiftly turned the amateur dabbler and dilettante into a serious philological scholar. Murray was introduced into membership of the august and exclusive Philological Society, no mean achievement for a young man who, it must be recalled, had left school at fourteen and had not thus far attended university. By 1869 he was on the Society's Council. In 1873 – having now left the bank and gone back to teaching at Mill Hill School – he published *The Dialect of the Southern Counties of Scotland*: it was a work that was to gild and solidify a reputation to the point of wide admiration (and to win him the invitation to contribute an essay on the history of English language for the ninth edition of the *Encyclopaedia Britannica*). It also brought him into contact with one of the most amazing men of Victorian England: the half-mad scholar-gypsy who was secretary of the Philological Society, Frederick Furnivall.

Some thought Furnivall – despite his devotion to mathematics, Middle English and philology – a total clown, an ass, a scandalous dandy and a fool (his critics, who were legion, made much of the fact that his father maintained a private lunatic asylum in the house where the young Frederick had grown up).

He was a Socialist, an agnostic and a vegetarian, and 'to alcohol and tobacco he was a stranger all his life'. He was a keen athlete, obsessed by sculling, and was particularly fond of teaching handsome young waitresses (recruited from the ABC teashop in New Oxford Street) the best way to get the most speed out of a slender racing boat he had designed. A photograph of him survives from 1901: he wears an impish smirk, not least because he is surrounded by eight pretty members of the Hammersmith Sculling Club for Girls, content and well-exercised women whose skirts may be long but whose shirts lie snug on their ample breasts. In the background stands a stern Victorian matron in her tough serge weeds, scowling.

For Frederick Furnivall was indeed an appalling flirt. He was condemned by many as socially reprehensible for committing the doubly unpardonable sin of marrying a lady's maid, and then abandoning her. Dozens of editors and publishers refused to work with him: he was 'devoid of tact or discretion . . . had a boyish frankness of speech which offended many and led him into unedifying controversies . . . his declarations of hostility to religion and to class distinctions were often unreasonable and gave pain'.

He was, however, a brilliant scholar and, like Murray, had an obsessive thirst for learning; among his friends and admirers he could count Alfred Lord Tennyson, Charles Kingsley, William Morris, John Ruskin – Minor's London mentor, it would later turn out – and the Yorkshire-born composer Frederick Delius. Kenneth Grahame, a fellow sculler who worked at the Bank of England, came duly under Furnivall's spell, wrote *Wind in the Willows* and painted Furnivall into the plot as the Water Rat. 'We learned 'em!' says Toad. 'We taught 'em,' corrects Rat. Furnivall may have been a cunning mischief-maker, but he was also often right.

He may have been Grahame's mentor, but he was a much more significant figure in Murray's life. As the latter's biographer was to say, admiringly, Furnivall was to Murray 'stimulating and persuasive, often meddlesome and exasperating, always a dynamic and powerful influence, eclipsing even James in his gusto for life'.

He was in many ways a Victorian's Victorian, an Englishman's Englishman – and a natural choice, as the country's leading philologist, to take a dominant role in the making of the great new dictionary that was then in the process of being constructed.

It was Furnivall's friendship with and sponsorship of Murray – as well as Murray's links with Sweet and Ellis – that was to lead, ultimately, to the most satisfactory event of all. This occurred on the afternoon of 26 April 1878, at which time James Augustus Henry Murray was invited to Oxford, to a room in Christ Church, Oxford, and to an awesome full meeting of the grandest minds in the land, the Delegates of the Oxford University Press.

They were a formidable group – the college Dean, Henry Liddell (whose daughter Alice had so captivated the Christ Church mathematician Charles Dodgson that he wrote an adventure book for her, set in Wonderland); Max Müller, the Leipzig philologist, Orientalist and Sanskrit scholar who now held Oxford's chair of Comparative Philology; the Regius Professor of History, William Stubbs, the man who was credited in Victorian times as having made the subject worthy of respectable academic pursuit; the Canon of Christ Church and classical scholar Edwin Palmer; the Warden of New College, James Sewell – and so on and so on.

High Church, High Learning, High Ambition: these were the Men who Counted, the architects of the great intellectual constructions that originated during England's haughtiest and most self-confident time. As Brunel was to bridges and railways, as Burton was to Africa and as Scott was soon to be to the Pole, so these men were the best, the makers of indelible monuments to learning: of the books that were to be the foundation of the great libraries all around the globe.

And they had a project, they said, in which Murray might well be very interested indeed. A project that, unwittingly for all concerned, was eventually to put Murray on a collision course with a man whose interests and whose piety were curiously congruent with his own.

At first blush Minor might seem to have been a man more marked by his differences from Murray than by such similarities as these. He was rich where Murray was poor. He was of high estate where Murray's condition was irredeemably, if respectably, low. And though he was of almost the same age – just three years separated them – he had been born both of a different citizenship and, as it happens, in a place that was almost as many thousands of miles away from Murray's British Isles as it was then thought prudent and practicable for ordinary people to reach.

Chapter Three

The Madness of War

---

lunatic ('l(j)uːnətɪk), *a.* [ad. late L. *lūnātic-us*, f.
L. *lūna* moon: see -ATIC. Cf. F. *lunatique*, Sp., It.
lunatico.] **A.** *adj.*
  1. Originally, affected with the kind of insanity that
was supposed to have recurring periods dependent on
the changes of the moon. In mod. use, synonymous
with INSANE; current in popular and legal language,
but not now employed technically by physicians.

Ceylon, the lushly overgrown tropical island which seems to hang
from India's southern tip like a teardrop – or a pear, or a pearl, or
even (say some) a Virginia ham – is regarded by priests of the
world's stricter religions as the place where Adam and Eve were
exiled, after their fall from grace. It is a Garden of Eden for sinners,
an island limbo for those who yield to temptation.

These days it is called Sri Lanka; once the Arab sea-traders called
it Serendib, and in the eighteenth century Horace Walpole created
a fanciful story about three princes who reigned there, and who
had the enchanting habit of stumbling across wonderful things
quite by chance. Thus was the English language enriched with the
word *serendipity*, without its inventor, who never travelled to the
East, really knowing why.

But as it happens he was more accurate than he could have ever
known. Ceylon is in reality a kind of post-lapsarian treasure-island,
where every sensual gift of the tropics is available, both to reward
temptation, and to beguile and charm. So there is cinnamon and
coconut, coffee and tea, there are sapphires and rubies, mangoes

and cashews, elephants and leopards, and everywhere a rich, hot, sweetly moist breeze, scented by the sea, by spices and by blossoms.

And there are the girls – young, chocolate-skinned, giggling naked girls with sleek wet bodies and rosebud nipples and long hair and coltish legs and with scarlet and purple petals folded behind their ears, who play in the white Indian Ocean surf and who run, quite without shame, along the cool wet sands on their way back home.

It was these nameless village girls – the likes of whom have frolicked naked in the Sinhalese surf for scores of years past, just as they still do now – that young William Chester Minor remembered most. It was these young girls of Ceylon, he said later, who had unknowingly set him on the spiral path to his eventually insatiable lust, to his incurable madness and to his final perdition. He had first noticed the erotic thrill of their charms when he was just thirteen years old: it was to inflame a shaming obsession with sexuality that inspired his senses and sapped his energies from that moment on.

Minor was born on the island in June 1834 – little more than three years before, and fully 5,000 miles to the east of James Murray, the man with whom he would soon become so inextricably linked. And in one respect – and one respect only – the lives of the two so widely separated families were similar: both the Murrays and the Minors were exceedingly pious.

Thomas and Mary Murray were members of the Congregationalist Church, clinging to the conservative ways of seventeenth-century Scotland with a group known as the Covenanters. Eastman and Lucy Minor were Congregationalists too, but of the more muscularly evangelical kind who dominated the American colonies, and whose views and beliefs were descended from those of the Pilgrim fathers. And although Eastman Strong Minor had learned the skills of printing and prospered as the owner of a press, his life eventually became devoted to taking the light of homespun American Protestantism into the dark interiors of the East Indies.

The Minors were in Ceylon as missionaries, and when William was born it was at the mission clinic, and into a devout mission family.

Unlike the Murrays, the Minors were first-line American aristocracy. The original settler in the New World was Thomas Minor, who came originally from the village of Chew Magna in western England. He had sailed across the Atlantic less than a decade after the Pilgrims, aboard a ship called the *Lion's Whelp*, which landed at Stonington, the port beside Mystic, at the mouth of Long Island Sound. Of the nine children born to Thomas and his wife Grace, six were boys, all of whom went on to spread the family name throughout New England, and be counted among the devout and high-principled founding fathers of the state of Connecticut in the late seventeenth century.

Eastman Strong Minor, who was born in Milford in 1809, was the head of the seventh generation of American Minors; the family members were by now generally prosperous, settled, respected. Few thought it other than a badge of honour when Eastman and his young Bostonian wife Lucy, whom he married in her city in 1833, closed down the family print shop and took off by steamer carrying a cargo of ice from Salem for Ceylon. Their piety was well known, and the Minor family seemed delighted that, in spite of the couple's wealth and social standing, they felt strongly enough in their calling to contemplate spending what would probably be many years away from America, preaching the Gospel to those regarded as less fortunate far away.

They arrived in Ceylon in March 1834, and were settled in the mission station in a village called Manepay, on the island's north-east coast, close to the great British naval station at Trincomalee. It was only three months later, in June, that William was born, his mother having suffered badly through the addition of sea-sickness to morning-sickness during the middle of her pregnancy. A second child, also named Lucy, was born two years later.

Although William's medical file suggests a typically rugged

Indian childhood – breaking a collar-bone in a fall from a horse, being knocked unconscious after falling from a tree, the usual slight doses of malaria and blackwater fever – his was far from a normal childhood.

His mother died of consumption when he was three. Two years later, instead of returning home to America with his two young children, Eastman Strong Minor set off on a journey through the Malay peninsula, bent on finding a second wife among the mission communities there. He left his little girl in charge of a pair of missionaries in a Sinhalese village called Oodooville, and took off on an eastbound tramp steamer with young William in tow.

The pair arrived in Singapore, where Minor had a mutual friend who introduced him to a party of American missionaries bound up-country to preach the Gospel in Bangkok. One of them was a handsome (and conveniently orphaned) divine named Judith Manchester Taylor, who came from Madison, New York. They courted, quickly, and tactfully out of sight of the curious child who had accompanied them. Minor persuaded Miss Taylor to come back with them on the next Jaffna-bound steamer, and they were married by the American Consul in Colombo shortly before Christmas 1839.

Judith Minor was as energetic as her printer-husband. She ran the local school, she learned Sinhalese, and taught it to her clearly very intelligent elder stepchild – as well as, in due course, to the six children of her own.

Two of the sons that resulted from this marriage died, the first aged one, the second aged five. One of William's half-sisters died when she was eight. His own sister Lucy died of consumption when she was twenty-one. (A third half-brother, Thomas T. Minor, died in peculiar circumstances many years later. He moved to the American West, first as doctor to the Winnebago tribe in Nebraska, then to the newly acquired Alaskan territory to collect specimens of Arctic habitations, and finally on to Port Townsend and Seattle, where he was elected mayor. In 1889, while still holding the post, he took off on a canoe expedition to Whidbey Island with a friend, G. Morris Haller. Neither man ever returned, and neither boats nor bodies were ever found. A Minor Street and a Thomas T. Minor School remain, as well as a reputation in Seattle that equates the name of Minor with some degree of glamour, pioneering and mystery.)

The mission library at Manepay was well stocked, and, though the accommodation for the family was 'very poor' according to Judith's diaries, the mission school itself was excellent – allowing young William to win a markedly better education than he might have received back in New England. His father's printing tasks gave him access to literature and newspapers; and his parents travelled by horse-and-buggy often, and took him along, and encouraged him to learn as many of the local languages as possible. By the time he was twelve he spoke good Sinhalese and claims to have had a fair grounding in Burmese, as well as some Hindi and Tamil and a smattering of various Chinese dialects. He also knew his way around Singapore, Bangkok and Rangoon, as well as the island of Penang, off the coast of what was then British Malaya.

William was just thirteen, he later told his doctors, when he first started to enjoy 'lascivious thoughts' about the young native girls on the sands around him: they must have seemed a rare constant in a shifting, inconstant life. But by the time he was fourteen, his parents (who were perhaps aware of his pubescent longings) decided to send him back to America, well away from the temptations of the tropics. He was to live with his uncle Alfred, who then ran a large crockery shop in the centre of New Haven. So William was seen off from Colombo port on one of the regular P & O liners that made the unendurably lengthy passage between Bombay and London – via (this was 1848, long before the completion of the Suez Canal) the long seas around the Cape of Good Hope.

He later admitted to vividly erotic recollections from the voyage. In particular he remembered being 'fiercely attracted' to a young

English girl who he met aboard ship. He seems not to have been warned that long tropical days and nights at sea, combined with the slow rocking motion of the swell, the tendency for women to wear short and light cotton dresses and for bartenders to offer exotic drinks, could very well, in those days as well as these, lead to romance – particularly if one or even both sets of parents were absent.

Much appears to have happened during the four weeks at sea – though not, perhaps, the ultimate. For the friendship appears to have gone unconsummated, no matter the time that the pair spent alone. Many years later Minor was to point out to his doctors that, as with his fantasies over the small Indian girls, he never let his sexual feelings for his fellow passenger get the better of him, nor ever 'gratified himself in an unnatural way'. Matters might have turned out very differently if he had.

Guilt – which is perhaps a frequent handmaiden among the peculiarly pious – seems to have intervened, even more than a teenager's shyness or natural caution. From this moment on in Minor's long and tormented life, sex and guilt come to appear firmly and fatally riveted together. He keeps apologizing to his questioners of later years: his thoughts were 'lascivious', he was 'ashamed' by them, he did his best not to 'yield'. He seems to have been looking over his shoulder all the time, making sure that his parents – perhaps the mother whom he lost when he was barely out of infancy, or perhaps the stepmother, so often the cause of problems for boy-children – never came to know the 'vile machinations', as he saw them, of his increasingly troubled mind.

But these feelings were still nascent in Minor's teenage years, and at the time he was unworried by them. He had his academic life to pursue, eagerly. From London he took another ship to Boston, and thence home to New Haven, where he began the arduous task of studying medicine at Yale University. His parents and their much diminished family were not to return for six more years, by which time he was twenty. He appears to have spent these, and indeed the following nine years of his medical apprenticeship, in quietly assiduous study, setting to one side what would soon become his deeper concerns.

He passed all his examinations without any apparent undue problems, and he graduated from Yale Medical School with a degree and a specialization in comparative anatomy in February 1863, when he was twenty-nine. The only recorded drama of those years came when he caught a serious infection after cutting his hand while conducting a post-mortem on a man who had died of septicaemia: he reacted quickly, painting his hand with iodine, but not quickly enough. He had been gravely ill, his doctors later said, and had nearly died.

By now he was a grown man, tempered by his years in the East and honed by his studies at what was then one of America's finest schools. Although he had no inkling that his mind was in so perilously fragile a state, he was about to embark on what was almost certainly the most traumatic period of his young life. He applied to join the army as a surgeon – an army that at the time was keenly short of medical personnel. For it was not just the army – it was then calling itself the Union Army: America, still young also, was then suffering the most traumatic period of her national life. The Civil War, the War between the States, was well under way.

When Minor signed his first contract with the army – which trained him conveniently close to home at the Knight Hospital in New Haven itself – the war was almost precisely halfway done, though naturally none knew this at the time. Eight hundred days of it had been fought so far: men had seen the battles of Forts Sumter, Clark, Hatteras and Henry, the First and Second Battles of Bull Run, the fights over patches of land at Chancellorsville, Fredericksburg, Vicksburg, Antietam, and over scores of otherwise unsung and unremembered trophies, like Mississippi's Big Black River Bridge, or Island Number Ten, Missouri, or Greasy Creek,

Kentucky. The South had so far had an abundance of victories: the Union Army, sorely pressed by years of bitter fighting and far too many reverses, would take all the men it could. It was eager to accept someone as apparently competent and well-Yankee-born as William Chester Minor of Yale.

Four days after he joined up, on 29 June 1863, came the Battle of Gettysburg, the bloodiest battle of the entire war, the turning-point, beyond which the Confederacy's military ambitions began to fail. The newspapers that Minor read each evening in New Haven were full of accounts of the progress of the fighting; there were 22,000 casualties on the Union side, and to those numbers even a tiny state like Connecticut contributed a monstrous share – it lost more than a quarter of the men it sent to Pennsylvania during the first three days in July, when the worst fighting took place. The world, President Lincoln was to say six months later when he consecrated the land as a memorial to the fallen, could never forget what they did there.

No doubt the tales of the battle stirred the young surgeon: there were casualties aplenty, abundant work for an energetic and ambitious young doctor to do, and besides, he was on what now looked very much like the winning side. By August he was fully sworn in to do the army's bidding, by November he was under formal contract to serve as an acting assistant surgeon, to do whatever the Surgeon-General's Department demanded. He was itching, his brother was to testify later, to be sent to the seat of battle.

But it was six more months before the army finally agreed and transferred him down South, close to the sounds of war. In New Haven he had spent a relatively easy time, taking care of men who had been brought well away from the trauma of fighting, men who were now healing, both in body and mind. But down in northern Virginia where he was first sent, all was very different.

Here the full horror of this cruel and fearsomely bloody conflict came home to him, suddenly, without warning. Here was an inescapable irony of the Civil War, not known in any conflict between man before or since: the fact that this was a war fought with new and highly effective weapons, machines for the mowing-down of men, but at a time when an era of poor and primitive medicine was just coming to an end. It was fought with the mortar and the musket and the Minié ball, though not with anaesthesia and sulphonamides and penicillin. The common soldier was thus in a poorer position than at any time before or after: he could be monstrously ill treated by all the new weaponry, and yet only moderately well treated with all the old medicine.

So in the field hospitals there was gangrene, amputation, filth, pain and disease — the appearance of pus in a wound was said by doctors to be 'laudable', the sign of healing. The sounds in the first-aid tents were unforgettable: the screams and whimperings of men whose lives had been ruined by cruel guns and in ferocious and ceaseless battles. Some 360,000 Union troops died in the war, and so did 258,000 Confederates — and for every one who died from the wounds caused by the new weapons, so two died from incidental infection and illness and poor hygiene.

To Minor this was all still terribly alien. He was, his friends at home would later say, a sensitive man — courteous to a fault, somewhat academic, rather too gentle for the business of soldiering. He read, painted in water-colours, played the flute. But Virginia in 1864 was no place for the genteel and mild-mannered. And although it is never quite possible to pinpoint whatever causes the eruption of madness in a man, there is at least some circumstantial suggestion in this case that it was an event, or a coincidence of events, that took place in 1864 in Virginia that finally did unhinge Minor, and pitch him over the edge into what in those unforgiving times was regarded as wholesale lunacy.

Given what we now know about the setting and the circum-stance of his first encounter with war, it does seem at least reasonable and credible to suppose that his madness, latent, hiding, hovering in the background, was properly triggered here. Something specific

seems to have happened in Virginia's Orange County early in May
1864, during the two days of the astonishingly bloody encounter
that has since come to be called the Battle of the Wilderness. This
was a fight to test the most sane of men: events took place during
those two days that were quite beyond human imagination.

It is not clear exactly why Minor went to the Wilderness – his
written orders in fact called for him to proceed from New Haven
to Washington and to the Medical Director's office, where he
would replace a doctor called Abbott, then working at an army
divisional hospital in Alexandria. He eventually did as he was
bidden – but first, and possibly on the specific orders of the Medical
Director, he went eighty miles to the south-west of the Union
capital into the field, where he would see, for the only time in his
career, real fighting.

The Battle of the Wilderness was the first working test of the
assumption that, with the Gettysburg victory in July 1863, the tide
of events in the Civil War truly had changed. The following
March, President Lincoln had placed all Union forces under the
command of General Ulysses S. Grant, who swiftly devised a
master plan that called for nothing less than the total destruction
of the Confederate Army. The dissipated and ill-organized campaigns of the weeks and months before – skirmishes here and there,
towns and forts captured and recaptured – meant nothing in terms
of coherent strategy: so long as the Confederate Army remained
intact and ready to fight, so Jefferson Davis's Confederacy
remained. Kill the secessionist army, Grant reasoned, and you kill
the secessionist cause.

This grand strategy got formally under way in May 1864, when
the great military machine that Grant had assembled for finishing
off the Confederate Army began to roll southwards from the
Potomac. The campaign triggered by this first sweep would eventually cut through Dixie like a scythe: Sherman would rage from
Tennessee through Georgia, Savannah would be captured, the

main Confederate forces would surrender at Appomattox a mere eleven months from the start of Grant's offensive, and the final fight of the five-year war would take place in Louisiana, at Shreveport, almost exactly a year after Grant began to move.

But the beginnings of the strategy were the most difficult, with the enemy at his least broken and most determined – and in few places in those early weeks was the battle more fiercely joined than on the campaign's first day. General Grant's men marched along the foothills of the Blue Ridge Mountains and, on the afternoon of 4 May, crossed the Rapidan River into Orange County. Here they met Robert E. Lee's Army of Northern Virginia: the subsequent fight, which began with the river-crossing and ended only when Grant's men made a flanking pass out towards Spotsylvania, cost some 27,000 lives, in just fifty hours of savagery and fire.

There are three distinct aspects of this enormous battle that appear to make it particularly important in the story of William Minor.

The first was the sheer and savage ferocity of the engagement and the pitiless conditions on the field where it was fought. The thousands of men who faced each other did so in a landscape that was utterly unsuited for infantry tactics. It was (and still is) a gently sloping kind of countryside, thickly covered with second-growth timber and impenetrably dense underbrush. There are tracts of swamp country, muddy and fetid, heavy with mosquitoes. In May it is dreadfully hot, and the foliage away from the swamps and seeping brooks is always tinder-dry.

The fighting therefore was conducted not with artillery – which couldn't see – nor with cavalry – which couldn't ride. It had to be conducted by infantrymen with muskets – their guns charged with the dreadful flesh-tearing Minié ball, a new-fangled kind of bullet that was expanded by a powder charge in its base and inflicted huge, unsightly wounds – or hand to hand, with bayonets and sabres. And with the heat and smoke of battle came yet another terror: fire.

The brush caught ablaze, and flames tore through the wilderness ahead of a stiff hot wind. Hundreds, perhaps thousands of men, the wounded as well as the fit, were burned to death, suffering the most terrible agonies.

One doctor wrote how soldiers appeared to have been wounded 'in every conceivable way, men with mutilated bodies, with shattered limbs and broken heads, men enduring their injuries with stoic patience, and men giving way to violent grief, men stoically indifferent, and men bravely rejoicing that – it is only a leg!' Such tracks as existed were jammed with crude wagons pulling blood-soaked casualties to the dressing stations, and overworked, sweating doctors tried their best to deal with injuries of the most gruesome kind.

A soldier from Maine wrote with appalled wonder of the fire. 'The blaze ran sparkling and crackling up the trunks of the pines, till they stood a pillar of fire from base to topmost spray. Then they wavered and fell, throwing up showers of gleaming sparks, while over all hung the thick clouds of dark smoke, reddened beneath by the glare of flames.' 'Forest fires raged,' wrote another soldier who was at the Wilderness, 'ammunition trains exploded; the dead were roasted in the conflagration; the wounded, roused by its hot breath, dragged themselves along with their torn and mangled limbs, in the mad energy of despair, to escape the ravages of the flames; and every bush seemed hung with shreds of bloodstained clothing. It seemed as though Christian men had turned to fiends, and hell itself had usurped the place of earth.'

The second aspect of the battle that may be important in understanding Minor's bewildering pathology relates to one particular group who played a part in the fighting: the Irish, the same Irish of whom Minor's London landlady later testified he appeared to be strangely frightened.

There were around 150,000 Irish soldiers on the Union side in the struggle, many of them subsumed anonymously into the Yankee units that happened to recruit where they lived. But there was also a proud assemblage of Irishmen who fought together, as a bloc: these were the soldiers of the 2nd Brigade, the Irish Brigade, and they were braver and rougher than almost any other unit in the entire Union Army. 'When anything absurd, forlorn, or desperate was to be attempted,' as one English war correspondent wrote, 'the Irish Brigade was called upon.'

The Brigade fought at the Wilderness: men of the 28th Massachusetts and the 116th Pennsylvania were there, alongside Irishmen from New York's legendary regiments, the 63rd, the 88th and the 69th – which still to this day leads the St Patrick's Day Parade up the green-lined expanse of Fifth Avenue every 17 March.

But there was a subtle difference in the mood of the Irishmen who fought with the Union troops in 1864, compared with those who had fought one or two years before. At the beginning of the war, before Emancipation had been proclaimed, the Irish were staunch in their support of the North, and equally antipathetic to a South that seemed, at least in those early days, backed by the British they so loathed. Their motives in fighting were complex – but once again a complexity that is important to this story. They were new immigrants from a famine-racked Ireland, and they were fighting in America not just out of gratitude to a country that had given them succour, but in order to be trained to fight back home one day, and to rid their island of the hated British once and for all. An Irish-American poem of the time made the point:

> When concord and peace to this land are restored,
> And the union's established for ever,
> Brave sons of Hibernia, oh, sheathe not the sword: –
> You will then have a union to sever.

The Irish were not to remain long in sympathy with all the Union aims. They were fierce rivals with American blacks, competing at the base of the social ladder for such opportunities – work, especially – as were on offer. And once the blacks were formally emancipated by Lincoln in 1863, the natural advantage that the Irish believed they had in the colour of their skins quite vanished – and with it much of their sympathy for the Union cause in the war they had chosen to fight. Besides, they had been doing their sums: 'We did not cause this war,' one of their leaders said, 'but vast numbers of our people have perished for it.'

The consequence was that – especially in battles where it seemed as though the Irish troops were being used as cannon-fodder – they began to leave the fields of battle. They began to desert. And large numbers of them certainly deserted from the terrible flames and bloodshed of the Battle of the Wilderness. It was desertion (and one of the particular punishments often inflicted on those convicted of it) that stands as the third and possibly the principal reason for Minor's subsequent fall.

Desertion, like indiscipline and drunkenness, was a chronic problem during the Civil War: seriously so because it deprived the commanders of the manpower they badly needed. It was a problem that grew as the war itself endured – the enthusiasm of the two causes abated as the months and years went on, and the numbers of casualties grew. The total strength of the Union Army was probably 2,900,000, and that of the Confederacy 1,300,000 – and, as we have seen, they suffered swingeing casualty totals of 360,000 and 258,000 respectively. The number of men who simply dropped their guns and fled into the forest is almost equally spectacular – 287,000 from the Union side, 103,000 from the South. Of course these figures are somewhat distorted: they represent men who fled, were captured and set to fighting again, only to desert once more, and perhaps many times subsequently. But they are still gigantic numbers – 10 per cent of the Union Army, one in twelve from the Rebels.

By the middle of the war more than 5,000 soldiers were deserting every month – some merely dropping behind during the interminable route marches, others fleeing in the face of gunfire. In May 1864 – the month when General Grant began his southern progress, and the month of the Wilderness – no fewer than 5,371 Union soldiers cut and ran. More than 170 left the field every day, both draftees and volunteers, and they may have run for any number of reasons: they may have been heartsick, homesick, depressed, bored, disillusioned, unpaid or just plain scared. Minor had not merely stumbled from the calm of Connecticut into a scene of carnage and horror: he had also come across a demonstration of man at his least impressive, fearful, depleted in spirit and cowardly.

Army regulations of the time were rather flexible when it came to prescribing penalties for drinking – a common punishment was to make the man stand on a box for several days, with a billet of wood on his shoulder – but they were unambiguous when it came to desertion. Anyone caught and convicted of 'the one sin which may not be pardoned in this world or the next' would be shot. That, at least, was what was said on paper: 'desertion is a crime punishable by death'.

But to shoot one of your own soldiers, whatever his crime, had a practical disbenefit – it diminished your own numbers, weakened your own forces. This piece of grimly realistic arithmetic persuaded most Civil War commanders, on both sides, to devise alternative punishments for those who ran away. Only a couple of hundred men were shot, though their deaths were widely publicized in a vain effort to set an example. Many were thrown into prison, locked in solitary confinement, flogged or heavily fined.

The rest – and most first-time offenders – were usually subjected to public humiliations of varying kinds. Some had their heads shaved, or half shaved, and were forced to wear boards with the inscription *Coward*. Some were sentenced by drumhead courts martial to a painful ordeal called *bucking*, in which the wrists were tied tightly, the arms forced over the knees and a stick secured between knees and arms – leaving the convict in an excruciating contortion, often for days at a time. (It was a punishment so harsh as to prove often decidedly counter-productive: one general who ordered a man to be bucked for straggling found that half his company deserted in protest.)

A man could also be gagged with a bayonet, which was tied across his open mouth with twine. He could be suspended from his thumbs, made to carry a yard of rail across his shoulders, be drummed out of town, forced to ride a wooden horse, made to walk around in a barrel-shirt and no other clothes – he could even, as in one gruesome case in Tennessee, be nailed to a tree and crucified.

Or else – and here it seemed, was the perfect combination of pain and humiliation – he could be *branded*. The letter 'D' would be seared on to his buttock, his hip or his cheek. It would be a letter one and a half inches high – the regulations were quite specific on this point – and it would either be burned on with a hot iron or cut with a razor and the wound filled with black-powder, to cause both irritation and indelibility.

For some unknown reason the regimental drummer-boy would often be employed to administer the powder; or, in the case of the use of a branding-iron, the doctor. And this, it was said at the London trial, was what Minor had been forced to do.

An Irish deserter, who had been convicted at drumhead of running away during the terrors of the Wilderness, was sentenced to be branded. The officers of the court – there would have been a colonel, four captains and three lieutenants – demanded in this case that the new young surgeon who had been assigned to them, this fresh-faced and genteel-looking aristocrat, this *Yalie*, fresh down from the hills of New England, be instructed to carry out the punishment. It would be as good a way as any, the old war-weary officers implied, to induct Minor into the rigours of war. And so the Irishman was brought to him, his arms shackled behind his back.

He was a dirty and unkempt man in his early twenties, his dark uniform torn to rags by his frantic, desperate run through the brambles. He was exhausted and frightened. He was like an animal – a far cry from the young lad who had arrived, cocksure and full of Dublin mischief, on the West Side of Manhattan three years before. He had seen so much fighting, so much dying – and yet now the cause for which he had fought was no longer truly his cause, not since Emancipation at least. His side was winning, anyway – they wouldn't be needing him any more, they wouldn't miss him if he ran away.

He wanted to be rid of his duties for the alien Americans. He wanted to go back home to Ireland. He wanted to see his family again, and be finished with this strange foreign conflict to which, in truth, he had never been more than a mercenary party. He wanted to use the soldiering skills he had learned in all those fights in Pennsylvania and Maryland and now in the fields of Virginia to fight against the British, despised occupiers of his homeland.

But now he had made the mistake of trying to run, and five soldiers from the Provost-Marshal's unit, on the look-out for him, had grabbed him from where he had been hiding behind the barn on a farm up in the foothills. The court martial had been assembled all too quickly and, as with all drumhead justice, the sentence was handed down in a brutally short time: he was to be flogged, thirty lashes with the cat – but only after being seared with a branding iron, the mark of desertion for ever to scar his face.

He pleaded with the court; he pleaded with his guards. He cried, he screamed, he struggled. But the soldiers held him down, and Minor took the hot iron from a basket of glowing coals that had been hastily borrowed from the brigade farrier. He hesitated for a moment – a hesitation that betrayed his own reluctance, for was this, he wondered briefly, truly permitted under the terms of his Hippocratic code? The officers grunted for him to continue – and he pressed the glowing metal on to the Irishman's cheek. The flesh sizzled, the blood bubbled and steamed, the prisoner screamed and screamed.

And then it was over. The wretch was led away, holding to his injured cheek the alcohol-soaked rag that Minor had given him. Perhaps the wound would become infected, would fill with the 'laudable pus' that other doctors said hinted at cure. Perhaps it would fester and crust with sores. Perhaps it would blister and burst and bleed for weeks. He didn't know.

All that he was sure of was that the brand would be with him for the rest of his life. In America it would mark him as a coward, as shaming a punishment as the court had decreed. Back home in Ireland it would mark him as something else altogether: it would single him out as a man who had gone to America to train with the army, and who was now back in Ireland, bent on fighting against the British authorities. He could clearly be identified, from now on, as a member of one of the Irish nationalist rebel groups – and every soldier and policeman in England and Ireland would recognize that, and would either lock him up to keep him off the streets, or would harass and harry him for every moment of his waking life.

His future as an Irish revolutionary was, in other words, quite over. He could care little for his ruined social standing in America; but for his future and now very vulnerable position in Ireland, where he had been marked and blighted for ever by the fact of one battlefield punishment, he was now bitterly angry. He realized that as an Irish patriot and revolutionary he was now useless, unemployable, worthless in all regards.

And in his anger he most probably felt, justly or not, that his ever more intense wrath should be directed against the man who had so betrayed his calling as a medical man, and had instead, and without objection, marked his face so savagely and incurably. He would have decided that he was and should be bitterly and eternally angry at Minor.

So he would go home, he vowed, just as soon as this war was over; and once home he would, the moment he stepped off the boat on the docks at Queenstown or Kingstown, tell all Irish patriots the following: William Chester Minor, American, was an enemy of all good Fenian fighting men, and revenge would be exacted from him, in good time and in due course.

This, at least, is what Minor almost certainly thought was in the mind of the man he had branded. Yes, it was later said, he had been terrified by his exposure to the battlefield, and 'exposure in the field' was suggested by some doctors as the cause of his ills; one story also had it that he had been present at the execution of a man – a Yale classmate, some reports had it, though none included a time or a place – and that he had been severely affected by what he had seen; but most frequently it was said he was fearful that Irishmen would abuse him shamefully, as he put it, and this was because he had been ordered to inflict so cruel a punishment on one of their number in America.

It was a story that was put about in court. Mrs Fisher, his landlady in Tenison Street had, according to the official court reports in *The Times*, suggested as much. The story was raised many times over the following decades, when people remembered that he was still locked up in an asylum, to account for his illness; and until 1915, when as an elderly man he gave an interview to a journalist in Washington, DC, and told quite another story, it remained one of the leading probable causes of his insanity. 'He branded an Irishman during the American Civil War,' they used to say. 'It drove him mad.'

A week or so later Minor, suffering no apparent short-term effects from his experience, was moved from under the red flag of the advanced field hospital (the red cross was not to be adopted by the United States until the ratification of the Geneva Convention, at the end of the Civil War) and sent to where he had been originally bound, the city of Alexandria.

He arrived there on 17 May, and went first to work at L'Overture Hospital, which was then reserved largely for black and so-called 'contraband' patients – escaped Southern slaves. There are records showing that he moved around the Union hospital system: he worked at Alexandria General Hospital, and at the Slough Hospital – and there is also a letter from his old military hospital in New

Haven, asking that he come back, since his work had been so good.

Demand like this was unusual, since Minor was labouring still at the lowliest rank of the war's medical personnel, as an acting assistant surgeon. In the course of the conflict there were 5,500 men contracted by the Union at this rank, and they included some devastating incompetents – graduates in botany and homeopathy, drunks who had failed in private practice, fraudsters who preyed upon their patients, men who had never been to medical school at all. Most would vanish from the army once the fighting was over; few would even dare hope for promotion, or a regular commission.

But Minor did. He seems to have flung himself into his work. Some of his old autopsy reports survive: they display neat handwriting, a confident use of the language, decisive declarations as to the cause of death. Most of the reports are forlorn: a sergeant from the 1st Michigan Cavalry dying of lung cancer, a common soldier dying of typhoid, another with pneumonia. These ailments were all too common in the days of Civil War medicine, and they were all treated with the ignorance of the day, with little more than the dual weapons of opium and calomel, pain-killer and purgative.

One report is more interesting. Written in September 1866, two years after the Battle of the Wilderness, it concerns a recruit, 'a stout muscular man' named Martin Kuster, who was struck by lightning while he was on sentry-go, imprudently standing under a poplar tree during a thunderstorm. He was in bad shape. 'The left side of his cap open . . . facing of the metal button torn off . . . hair of his left temple singed and burned . . . stocking and right boot torn open . . . a faint yellow and amber colored line extended down his body . . . burns down to his pubis and scrotum.'

This report did not come from Virginia, however; nor was it written by an acting assistant surgeon. It came instead from Governors Island, New York, and it was signed by Minor in his new capacity as an assistant surgeon, as a regular soldier in the United

States Army. By the autumn of 1866 he was no longer a contract-
man, but instead enjoyed the full rank of a commissioned captain.
He had done what most of his colleagues had failed to do: by
dint of hard work and scholarship, and by using his Connecticut
connections to the full, he had made the transition into the upper
ranks of America's regular army officers.

His supporters, in Connecticut and elsewhere, were unaware
of any incipient madness: Professor James Dana – a Yale geologist
and mineralogist whose classic textbooks are still in use today –
said that Minor was 'one of the half dozen best . . . in the country',
and that his appointment as an army surgeon 'would be for the
good of the Army and the honor of the country'. Another professor
wrote of him as 'a skillful physician, an excellent operator, an
efficient scholar' – although, adding what might later be interpreted
as a tocsin note, remarked that his moral character was 'unexcep-
tional'.

Just before his formal examination Minor had signed a form
declaring that he did not labour under any 'mental or physical
infirmity of any kind, which can in any way interfere with the
most efficient duties in any climate'. His examiners agreed: in
February 1866 they granted him his commission and by mid-
summer he was on Governors Island, dealing with one of the
major emergencies of the post-war period: the fourth and last of
the East's great cholera epidemics.

It was said that the illness was brought in by Irish immigrants
who were then pouring in through Castle Clinton: some 1,200
people died during the summertime scourge, and the hospitals and
clinics on Governors Island were filled with the sick and the
isolated. Minor worked tirelessly throughout the months of the
plague, and his work was recognized: by the end of the year,
though still nominally a lieutenant, he was breveted with the rank
of captain, as reward for his services.

But at the same time there came disturbing signs in Minor's
behaviour of what in hindsight now appears to have been incipient

paranoia. He began to carry a gun when he was out of uniform. Quite illegally, he took along his Colt .38 service revolver, with a six-shot spinning magazine that, according to custom, had one of the chambers blocked off with a permanent blank. He carried the weapon, he explained, because one of his fellow officers had been killed by muggers when returning from a bar in lower Manhattan. He might be followed by ruffians, he said, who might try to attack him too.

He started to become a *habitué* of the wilder bars and brothels of the Lower East Side and Brooklyn. He embarked on a career of startling promiscuity, sleeping night after night with whores, and returning to Fort Jay Hospital on Governors Island by rowboat, in the early hours of the next morning. His colleagues became alarmed: this was totally out of character, it seemed, for so gentle and studious an officer – and particularly so when it became clear that he frequently needed treatment, or such as was available, for a variety of venereal infections.

In 1867, the year when his father Eastman died in New Haven, he surprised his colleagues by suddenly announcing his engagement to a young woman who lived in Manhattan. Neither she nor her job has been identified – but the suspicion is that she was a dancer or an entertainer, met on one of his tenderloin expeditions. The girl's mother, however, was not as impressed with Minor as his Connecticut friends had been. She detected something unsavoury about the young captain, and insisted that her daughter break the engagement, which she eventually did. In later years Minor refused adamantly to discuss the affair, or to say how he felt about its forced conclusion. His doctors said that he appeared embittered about the episode.

The army, meanwhile, was dismayed by what seemed the sudden change in their protégé. Within weeks of learning of his extraordinary behaviour the Surgeon-General's Department decided to remove him from the temptations of New York and send him out of harm's way, into the countryside. They effectively demoted him, in fact, by ordering him to the relative isolation of the obscure Fort Barrancas, Florida. The fort, which guards Pensacola Bay on the Gulf of Mexico, was already becoming obsolete. It was an elderly masonry structure built to protect the bay and its port from foreign raiders: and it now housed only a small detachment of troops, to whom Minor became regimental doctor. For a man so well born, so educated, so full of promise, this was a truly humiliating situation.

He become furiously angry with the army. He clearly missed his debauches; his mess-mates noticed that he became moody, occasionally very aggressive. In his quieter moments he took up his paintbrushes: water-colours of the Florida sunsets soothed him, he said. He still was a dab hand, according to his brother officers. He was an artistic man, commented one in particular. He seemed like someone with a soul.

But he then began to harbour suspicions about his fellow soldiers. He thought they were muttering about him, glancing suspiciously at him all the time. One officer troubled Minor, began teasing him, goading him, persecuting him in ways that Minor would never discuss. He challenged the man to a duel, and had to be reprimanded by the fort commander. The officer was one of Minor's best friends, said the commander – and both he and the friend later said they were incredulous that they had fallen out so badly, for no obvious reason. Nothing anyone could do to explain – that your best friend is not plotting against you, is not scheming, is not wanting to have you hurt – nothing seemed to get through. Minor seemed to have taken leave of his senses. It was all very puzzling and, to his friends and family, deeply distressing.

It reached a climax during the summer of 1868, when, after reportedly staying too long in the Florida sun, he began to complain of severe headaches and terrible vertigo. He was sent with escorting nurses to New York, to report to his old unit and to his old doctor. He was interviewed, examined, prodded, pried. By September it was perfectly plain to see he was seriously unwell. For the first time suspicion turned to certainty, with a formal indication that his mind had started to falter.

A paper signed by a Surgeon Hammond on 3 September 1868 states that Minor appeared to be suffering from *monomania* – a form of insanity that involves a fierce obsession with just a single topic. What that topic was Surgeon Hammond does not report, but he does say that, in his view, Minor's condition was so serious that he was to be classified as 'delusional'. Minor was just thirty-four years old: his life and his mind had begun to veer out of control.

The sick notes began to pile up, week after week. 'He is in my opinion, unfit for duty and not able to travel,' they each declared. By November the doctors were recommending a more drastic step: Minor should in the army's opinion be immediately institutionalized. He should, moreover, be put in the charge of the celebrated Dr Charles Nichols, the Superintendent of the Government Hospital for the Insane in Washington, D C.

'The monomania,' said the examining doctor, in a letter written in suitably magnificent copperplate, 'is now decidedly suicidal and homicidal. Dr Minor has expressed willingness to go to the Asylum, and has said he hoped he would be permitted to go without a guard, which I think he is now fully capable of doing.'

Capable, but ashamed. A letter, begging permission on Minor's behalf for him to go to the asylum without people knowing, survives. 'He shrinks from what he regards as the stigma of medical treatment in a lunatic asylum. He does not know that I write this. He would be grateful to anyone whose influence would place him under medical treatment in the Asylum without its being generally known.'

The letter worked, the influence of the old family, the old school, proved effective. A day later, without a guard and in secret, Minor took the express train down through Philadelphia and Wilmington and Baltimore to Union Station, Washington. He took a hansom cab to south-east Washington, and to the well-tended grounds of the hospital. He passed through the stone gates, to begin what would become a lifelong acquaintance with the insides of lunatic asylums.

The Washington institution would eventually be renamed St Elizabeth's in 1916, and become infamous: Ezra Pound would be detained there, as would John Hinckley, Jr, the attempted assassin of President Reagan. For the balance of the nineteenth century, however, the institution would be known more anonymously, as the only government-run site in the country in which soldiers and sailors who had gone certifiably mad could be detained, rehabilitated, locked away. Minor was to remain there for the next eighteen months. He was a trusted inmate, however: the superintendent allowed him free run of the grounds, then let him go unescorted into the nearby countryside – a century and a half ago Washington was a very different place, fields where there are now slums. He walked into town; he passed by the White House; he visited the pay office each month and drew his salary in cash.

But he remained beset by delusional fears. A team of army doctors visited him the following September. 'Our observations lead us to form a very unfavorable opinion as to Dr Minor's condition,' they told the Surgeon-General. 'A very long time may elapse before he can possibly be restored to health.' Another doctor concurred: 'The disturbance of the cerebral function is ever more marked.'

The following April his commanders reached an unoptimistic decision: Minor was never likely to be cured, they said, and should be formally placed on the Army Retired List. A hearing was held in the Army Building at the corner of Houston and Greene Streets, in what is now New York's fashionably bohemian area of SoHo, to formalize the soldier's retirement, and to make sure it was justified by circumstance.

It was a protracted, sad affair. A brigadier, two colonels, a major and a surgeon-captain sat on the board, and they listened silently as doctor after doctor gave evidence about this once so promising young man's decline. Perhaps the mental condition from which he was suffering had been caused by exposure to the sun in Florida, said one; perhaps it had been merely aggravated by it, said another; perhaps it was all due to the man's exposure to war, a consequence of the horrors that he had witnessed.

No matter precisely how the madness was precipitated, the board eventually reached what was the only proper conclusion on how to deal with it, administratively. In the official view of the army, Brevet Captain Assistant William C. Minor was now wholly 'incapacitated by causes arising in the line of duty' – the crucial phrase of the ruling – and should be retired with immediate effect.

He was, in other words, one of the walking wounded. He had served his country, he had been ruined by serving so, and his country owed him a debt. If the beguiling eroticisms of Ceylon, his tragic family circumstances, his obsessive cravings for whores, his *nostalgie de la boue* – if any or all of these factors had ever played a part in his steady mental decline, then so be it. The line of duty had done for him. The United States Army would now look after him. He was a ward of Uncle Sam. He could be designated by the honorific phrase after his name, *US Army, Ret'd*. His pay and pension would remain – and in fact they did so, for the rest of his life.

In February 1871 a friend in New York writes to report that Minor had been released from the asylum, and was on his way to Manhattan, to stay with a medical friend on West 20th Street. A few weeks later he was said to have gone home to New Haven, to spend the summer with his brother Alfred, to see his old friends at Yale, and to busy himself in his late father's emporium – Minor & Co., Dealers in China, Glass and Crockery – which Alfred and his older brother George ran at 261 Chapel Street. The summer and autumn days of 1871 were among the last free and tranquil American days that Minor was ever to enjoy.

In October, with the red and golden leaves of the New England trees already beginning to fall, Minor boarded a steamer in Boston, with a single ticket to the Port of London. He planned to spend a year or so in Europe, he told his friends. He would rest, read, paint. Perhaps he would visit a spa or two, he would see Paris and Rome and Venice, he would refresh and reinvigorate what he well knew was a troubled mind. One of his friends at Yale had written a letter of introduction to Mr Ruskin: he would doubtless be able to charm the artistic *demi-monde* of the British capital. He was, after all – and how many times had he heard the phrase at the army hearings – 'a gentleman of Christian refinement, taste and learning'. He would take London by storm. He would recover. He would return to America a new man.

He stepped off the boat on a foggy morning in early November. He offered his identification as an officer in the United States Army to the officials in the customs shed, and took a landau to Radley's Hotel, near Victoria Station. He had money with him. He had his books, his easel, his water-colours, his brushes.

And he also had, secure in its japanned box, his gun.

Chapter Four

Gathering Earth's Daughters

---

sesquipedalian (ˌsɛskwɪpɪ'deɪlɪən), *a.* and
sb [f. T.. *sesquipedālis*: see SESQUIPEDAL and -IAN.]
    A. *adj.* **1.** Of words and expressions (after Horace's
sesquipedalia verba 'words a foot and a half long', A.P.
97): Of many syllables.
    B. *sb.* **1.** A person or thing that is a foot and a half
in height or length.
    1615 *Curry-Combe for Coxe-Combe* iii. 113 He thought fit
by his variety, to make you knowne for a viperous Sesquipedalian in euery coast . . .
    2. A sesquipedalian word.
    1830 *Fraser's Mag.* I. 350 What an amazing power in writing
down hard names and sesquipedalians does not the following
passage manifest! **1894** *Nat. Observer* 6 Jan. 194/2 His sesquipedalians recall the utterances of another Doctor.
    Hence **sesquipe'dalianism,** style characterized by
the use of long words; lengthiness . . .

It was also on a foggy day in November, nearly fifteen years earlier, when the central events on the other side of this curious conjunction got properly under way. But while Minor arrived in London on a wintry November morning, and took himself to an unfashionable lodging-house in Victoria, this very different set of events took place early on a wintry November evening, and did so in an exceedingly select quarter of Mayfair.

The date was 5 November, Guy Fawkes' Day, 1857, the time was shortly after six, and the place a narrow terraced house at the north-west corner of one of London's most fashionable and aristocratic oases, St James's Square. On all sides were the grand town houses and private clubs of the extraordinary number of bishops and peers and Members of Parliament who lived there.

The finest shops in town were just a stone's throw away, as well as the prettiest churches, the most splendid office apartments, the oldest and most haughty of foreign embassies. The corner building on St James's Square housed an institution that was central to the intellectual lives of the great men who lived near by (a role it still plays today, though happily for a somewhat more democratic world). It provided accommodation for what its admirers regarded then, as they still do today, the finest private collection of publicly accessible books in the world, the London Library.

The Library had moved there twelve years before, from cramped quarters on Pall Mall. The new building was tall and capacious, and although today it is filled to bursting with many more than a million books, back in 1857 it had only a few thousand volumes, and had plenty of space to spare. So its committee decided early on to raise extra money by renting out rooms, though only, it was decreed, to societies whose adherents were likely to share the same lofty aims of scholarship as did the Library itself, and whose members would be able to mingle happily with the aristocratic, and often staggeringly snobbish, gentlemen who made up the Library's own membership rolls.

Two groups were chosen: the Statistical Society was one, the Philological Society the other. It was at a fortnightly meeting of the latter, held in an upstairs room on that chill Thursday evening, when words were spoken that were to set in train a most remarkable series of events.

The speaker was the Dean of Westminster, a formidable cleric by the name of Richard Chenevix Trench. Perhaps more than any other man alive, Dr Trench personified the sweepingly noble ambitions of the Philological Society. He firmly believed, as did most of its 200 members, that some kind of divine ordination lay behind what seemed then the ceaseless dissemination of the English language around the planet.

God – who in this part of London society was held to be an Englishman – naturally approved the spread of the language as an essential imperial device; but He also encouraged its undisputed corollary, which was the worldwide growth of Christianity. The equation was really very simple, a formula for undoubted global good: the more English there was in the world, the more God-fearing its peoples would be. (And for a Protestant cleric there was a useful subtext: if English did manage eventually to outstrip the linguistic influences of the Roman Church, then its reach might even help bring the two Churches back into some kind of ecumenical harmony.)

So even though the Society's stated role was academic, its informal purpose, under the direction of divines like Trench, was much more robustly chauvinist. True, earnestly classical philological discussions, of obscure topics like 'sound-shifts in the Papuan and Negrito dialects' or 'the role of the explosive fricative in High German', did lend scholarly heft to the Society, which was all very well. But the principal purpose of the group was in fact improving the understanding of what all members regarded as the properly dominant language of the world, and that was their own.

Sixty members were assembled at six o'clock on that November evening. Darkness had fallen on London soon after half past five. The gas lamps fizzed and sputtered, and on the corners of Piccadilly and Jermyn Street small boys were collecting last-minute pennies for fireworks, their ragged models of old Guy Fawkes, soon to be burned on bonfires, propped up before them. Already in the distance the whistles and crashes and hisses of exploding rockets and roman candles could be heard, as the early parties got under way.

Like the fire-frightened housemaids who hurried back down to the servants' entrances of the great houses near by, the old philologists, cloaked against the chill, scuttled through the gloom. They were men who had long since grown beyond such energetic diversions. They were eager to get away from the sound of explosions and the excitement of celebration, and repair to the calm of scholarly discourse.

Moreover, the topic for their evening's entertainment looked promising, and not in the least bit taxing. Trench was to discuss, in a two-part lecture that had been billed as of considerable importance, the subject of Dictionaries. The title of his talk suggested a bold agenda: he would tell his audience that the few dictionaries then in existence suffered from a number of serious shortcomings – grave deficiencies from which the language and, by implication, the Empire and its Church might well eventually come to suffer. For those Victorians who accepted the sturdy precepts of the Philological Society, this was just the kind of talk they liked to hear.

The English dictionary, in the sense that we commonly use the phrase today – as an alphabetically arranged list of English words, together with an explanation of their meanings – is a relatively new invention. Four hundred years ago there was no such convenience available on any English bookshelf.

There was none available, for instance, when William Shakespeare was writing his plays. Whenever he came to use an unusual word, or to set a word in what seemed an unusual context – and his plays are extraordinarily rich with examples – he had almost no way of checking the propriety of what he was about to do. He was not able to reach into his bookshelves and select any one volume to help; he would not be able to find any book that might tell him if the word he had chosen was properly spelled, whether he had selected it correctly or had used it in the right way in the proper place. Shakespeare was not even able to perform a function that we consider today as perfectly normal and ordinary a function as reading itself. He could not, as the saying goes, *look something up*. Indeed the very phrase – when it is used in the sense of *searching for something in a dictionary or encyclopaedia or other book of reference* – simply did not exist. It does not appear in the English language in fact until as late as 1692, when an Oxford historian named Anthony Wood used it (and died three years later).

Since there was no phrase until the late seventeenth century, it follows that there was essentially no concept either, certainly not at the time that Shakespeare was writing: a time when writers were writing furiously, and thinkers thinking as they had rarely done before. Despite all the intellectual activity of the time, there was in print no guide to the tongue, no linguistic vade-mecum, no single book that Shakespeare or Marlowe or Nashe, Francis Drake, John Donne or Ben Jonson, Walter Ralegh, Izaak Walton or Martin Frobisher or any of their other learned contemporaries could consult.

Consider, for instance, Shakespeare's writing of *Twelfth Night*, which he completed some time at the very beginning of the seventeenth century. Consider the moment, probably in the summer of 1601, when he has reached the writing of the scene in the Third Act in which Sebastian and Antonio, the shipwrecked sailor and his rescuer, have just arrived in port, and are wondering where they might stay the night. Sebastian considers the question for a moment, and then, in the manner of someone who has read and well remembered his *Good Hotel Guide* of the day, declares quite simply

> In the south suburbs, at the Elephant
> Is best to lodge . . .

Now what, exactly, did William Shakespeare know about elephants? Moreover, what does he know of Elephants as hotels? The name was one that was given to a number of lodging-houses in various cities dotted around Europe. This particular Elephant, given that this was *Twelfth Night*, happened to be in Illyria; but there were many others, two of them at least in London. But however many there were – just why was this the case? Why name an inn after such a beast? And what was such a beast anyway? All of these are questions that, one would think, a writer should at least *be able* to have answered.

Yet they were not. If Shakespeare did not happen to know very much about elephants, which was likely, and if he were unaware of this curious habit of naming hotels after them, where could he go to look up the question? And more, if he wasn't precisely sure that he was giving his Sebastian the proper reference for his lines — for was the inn really likely to be named after an elephant, or was it perhaps named after another animal, a camel or a rhino, or a gnu? — where could he look, to make quite sure? Where would a playwright of Shakespeare's time look up any word?

One might think he would want to look things up all the time. *Am not I consanguineous?* he writes in the same play. In the next scene he talks of *thy doublet of changeable taffeta*. He then says: *Now is the woodcock near the gin*. Shakespeare's vocabulary was evidently prodigious; but how could he be certain that in all the cases where he employed unfamiliar words, he was grammatically and factually right? What prevented him, to nudge him forward by a couple of centuries, becoming an occasional Mrs Malaprop?

The questions are worth posing simply to illustrate what we would now think of as the profound inconvenience of his not once being able to refer to a dictionary. At the time he was writing there were atlases aplenty, there were prayer-books, missals, histories, biographies, romances, books of science and art. Shakespeare is thought to have drawn many of his classical allusions from a specialized thesaurus that had been compiled by a man named Thomas Cooper — its many errors are replicated far too exactly in the plays for it to be coincidence — and he is thought also to have drawn from Thomas Wilson's *Arte of Rhetorique*. But that was all: there were no other literary and linguistic and lexical conveniences available at all.

It is perhaps difficult to imagine so creative a mind as Shakespeare's working without any lexicographical reference book beside him other than Mr Cooper's crib (which Mrs Cooper once threw into the fire, prompting the great man to begin all over again) and Mr Wilson's little manual; yet that was the condition under which his particular genius was compelled to flourish. The English language was spoken and written, but at the time of

Shakespeare it was not defined, not *fixed*. It was like the air: it was taken for granted, the medium that enveloped and defined all Britons. As to exactly what it was, what its components were – who knew?

That is not to say there were no dictionaries at all. There had been a collection of Latin words published as a *Dictionarius* as early as 1225, and a little more than a century later another, also Latin-only, as a helpmeet for students of St Jerome's difficult translation of the Scriptures known as the Vulgate. In 1538 the first of a series of Latin English dictionaries appeared in London: Thomas Elyot's alphabetically arranged list, which happened to be the first book to employ the English word *dictionary* in its title. Almost twenty years later a man named John Withals put out *A Shorte Dictionarie for Yonge Begynners* in both languages, but with the words arranged not alphabetically but by subject, as 'the names of Byrdes, Byrdes of the Water, Byrdes about the house, as cockes, hennes, etc., of Bees, Flies, and others'.

But what was still wanted was a proper English dictionary, a full statement of the extent of the English tongue. With one single exception, of which Shakespeare probably did not know when he died in 1616, his want remained stubbornly unfulfilled. Others were to remark on the apparent lack as well. Shortly before Shakespeare's death his friend John Webster wrote *The Duchess of Malfi*, incorporating a scene in which the Duchess's brother Ferdinand imagines that he is turning into a wolf, 'a very pestilent disease . . . They call lycanthropia'. 'What's that?' cries one of the cast. 'I need a dictionary to't!'

But in fact someone, a Rutland schoolmaster named Robert Cawdrey, who later moved to teach in Coventry, had evidently been listening to this drumbeat of demand. He read and took copious notes from all the reference books of the day, and eventually produced a first half-hearted attempt at what was wanted by publishing such a list in 1604 (the year Shakespeare probably wrote *Measure for Measure*).

It was a small octavo book of 120 pages, which Cawdrey titled *A Table Alphabeticall . . . of Hard Unusual English Words*. It had about 2,500 word-entries. He had compiled it, he said, 'for the benefit & help of Ladies, gentlewomen or any other unskilful persons. Whereby they may more easilie and better vnderstand many hard English wordes, which they shall heare or read in the Scriptures, Sermons or elsewhere, and also be made able to vse the same aptly themselues'. It had many shortcomings, but it was without doubt the very first true monolingual English dictionary, and its publication remains a pivotal moment in the history of English lexicography.

For the next century and a half there was a great flurry of commercial activity in the field, and dictionary after dictionary thundered off the presses, each one larger than the last, each boasting of superior value in the educating of the uneducated (among whom were counted the women of the day, who enjoyed little schooling compared to the men).

For all of the seventeenth century these books tended to concentrate, as Cawdrey's first offering had, on what were called 'hard words' – words that were not in common everyday use, or else words that had been invented specifically to impress others, the so-called *inkhorn terms* with which books of the sixteenth and seventeenth centuries seem well larded. Thomas Wilson, whose *Arte of Rhetorique* had helped Shakespeare, published examples of the high-flown style, such as that from a clergyman in Lincolnshire writing to a government official, begging a promotion:

There is a Sacerdotall dignitie in my native Countrey contiguate to me, where I now contemplate: which your worshipfull benignitie could sone impenetrate for mee, if it would like you to extend your sedules, and collaude me in them to the right honourable lord Chaunceller, or rather Archgrammacian of Englande.

The fact that the volumes concentrated on only the small section of the national vocabulary that encompassed such nonsense might

seem today to render them bizarrely incomplete, but back then
their editorial selection was regarded as a virtue. Speaking and
writing thus was the highest ambition of the English smart set.
'We present for you,' trumpeted the editor of one such volume
to would-be members, 'the choicest words.'

So, fantastic linguistic creations like *abequitate*, *bulbulcitate* and
sullevation appeared in these books alongside *Archgrammacian* and
contiguate, with lengthy definitions; there were words like *necessi-
tude*, *commotrix* and *parentate* – all of which are now listed, if listed
at all, as *obsolete* or *rare*, or both. Pretentious and flowery inventions
adorned the language – perhaps not all that surprising, considering
the flowery fashion of the times, with its perukes and powdered
periwigs, its rebatos and doublets, its ruffs and ribbons and scarlet
velvet Rhinegraves. So words like *adminiculation*, *cautionate*, *derunci-
nate* and *attemptate* are placed in the vocabulary too, each duly
catalogued in the tiny leather books of the day; yet they were
words meant only for the ears of the high-flown, and were unlikely
to impress Cawdrey's intended audience of ladies, gentlewomen
and 'unskilful persons'.

The definitions offered by these books were generally
unsatisfactory too. Some offered mere one-word or barely illumi-
nating synonyms – *magnitude*: 'greatness', or *ruminate*: 'to chew
over again, to studie earnestly upon'. Sometimes the definitions
were simply amusing: Henry Cockeram's *The English Dictionarie*
of 1623 defines *commotrix* as 'a Maid that makes ready and vnready
her Mistris', while *parentate* is 'to celebrate ones parents funerals'. Or
else the creators of these hard-word books put forward explanations
that were complex beyond endurance, as in a book called *Glossogra-
phia* (1656) by Thomas Blount, which offers as its definition of
shrew: 'a kind of Field-Mouse, which if he goes over a beasts back,
will make him lame in the Chine; and if he bite, the beast swells
to the heart, and dyes . . . From hence came our English phrase,
I beshrew thee, when we wish ill; and we call a curst woman a
Shrew.'

Yet in all of this lexicographical sound and fury – seven major dictionaries had been produced in seventeenth-century England, the last having no fewer than 38,000 headwords – two matters were being ignored.

The first was the need for a good dictionary to encompass the language *in its entirety*, the easy and popular words as well as the hard and obscure, the vocabulary of the common man as well as that of the learned house, the aristocrat and the rarefied school. Everything should be included: the mite of a two-letter preposition should have no less standing in an ideal word-list than the majesty of a piece of polysyllabic sesquipedalianism.

The second matter that dictionary-makers were ignoring was the coming recognition elsewhere that, with Britain and her influence now beginning to flourish in the world – with daring sailors like Drake and Ralegh and Frobisher skimming the seas, and with European rivals bending before the might of British power, and with new colonies securely founded in the Americas and India, which spread the English language and English concepts far beyond the shores of England – English was trembling on the verge of becoming a global language. It was starting to be an important vehicle for the conduct of international commerce and arms and law. It was displacing French and Spanish and Italian, and the courtly languages of foreigners; it needed to be far better known, far better able to be learned properly. An inventory needed to be made, of what was spoken, what was written, and what was read.

The Italians, the French and the Germans were already well advanced in securing their own linguistic heritage, and had gone so far as to ordain institutions to maintain their languages in fine fettle. In Florence, the Accademia della Crusca had been founded in 1582, dedicating itself to maintaining 'Italian' culture, even though it would be three centuries before there was a political entity called Italy. But there was a dictionary of Italian produced by the Accademia in 1612: the linguistic culture was alive, if not the country. In Paris the Cardinal de Richelieu had established the Académie

Française in 1634. The Forty Immortals – rendered in more sinister fashion as simply 'The Forty' – have presided over the integrity of the tongue with magnificent inscrutability to this day.

But the British had taken no such approach. It was in the eighteenth century that the impression grew that the nation needed to know in more detail what their language was, and what it meant. The English at the close of the seventeenth century, it was said, were 'uncomfortably aware of their backwardness in the study of their own tongue'. From then on the air was full of schemes for bettering the English language, for giving it greater prestige both at home and abroad.

Dictionaries improved, and very markedly so, during the first half of the new century. The most notable of them, a book that did indeed expand its emphasis from mere hard words to a broad swathe of the entire English vocabulary, was edited by a Stepney boarding-school owner named Nathaniel Bailey. Very little is known about him, other than his membership of the Seventh-day Baptist Church. But the breadth of his scholarship, the scope of his interest, is amply indicated by the title-page of his first edition (there were to be twenty-five of them between 1721 and 1782, all best-sellers). The page also hints at the quite formidable task that lay ahead of any drudge who might be planning to create a truly comprehensive English lexicon. Bailey's work was entitled:

A Universal Etymological Dictionary, Comprehending The Derivations of the Generality of Words in the English tongue, either Antient or Modern, from the Antient British, Saxon, Danish, Norman and Modern French, Teutonic, Dutch, Spanish, Italian, Latin, Greek and Hebrew Languages, each in their proper Characters. And Also A brief and clear Explication of all difficult Words . . . and Terms of Art relating to Botany, Anatomy, Physick . . . Together with A Large Collection and Explication of Words and Phrases us'd in our Antient Statutes, Charters, Writs, Old Records and Processes at Law; and the Etymology and Interpretation of the Proper Names of Men, Women and Remarkable Places in Great Britain: also the Dialects of our

Different Counties. Containing many Thousand Words more than . . . any English Dictionary before extant. To which is Added a Collection of our most Common Proverbs, with their Explication and Illustration. The whole work compil'd and Methodically digested, as well as for the Entertainment of the Curious as the Information of the Ignorant, and for the Benefit of young Students, Artificers, Tradesmen and Foreigners.

Good the volumes and the effort may have been, but still not quite good enough. Nathaniel Bailey and those who tried to copy him in the first half of the eighteenth century laboured mightily, though the task of corralling the entire language became ever larger the more it was considered: yet still no one seemed intellectually capable enough, or brave enough, or dedicated enough, or simply possessed of enough time to make a truly full record of the entire English language. And that, though no one seemed able even to say so, was what was really wanted. An end to timidity, to pussy-footing. The replacement of the philologically tentative by the lexicographically decisive.

And then came the man whom Smollett called Literature's Great Cham, and one of the most eminent literary figures of all time, Samuel Johnson. He decided to take up the challenge before which so many others had flinched. And even with the critical judgement of the more than two centuries since, it can fairly be said that what he created was an unparalleled triumph. Johnson's *A Dictionary of the English Language* was, and has remained ever since, a portrait of the language of the day, in all its majesty, beauty and marvellous confusion.

Few are the books that can offer so much pleasure, to look at, to hold, to skim, to read. They can still be found today, often cased in boxes of brown morocco. They are hugely heavy, built for the lectern rather than for the hand. They are bound in rich brown leather, the paper is thick and creamy, the print impressed deep into the weave. Few who read the volumes today can fail to be charmed by the quaint elegance of the definitions, of which Johnson was a master. Take for example the word for which Shakespeare might have hunted, *elephant*. It was, Johnson declared:

The largest of all quadrupeds, of whose sagacity, faithfulness, prudence and even understanding, many surprising relations are given. This animal is not carnivorous, but feeds on hay, herbs and all sorts of pulse; and it is said to be extremely long lifed. It is naturally very gentle: but when enraged, no creature is more terrible. He is supplied with a trunk, or long hollow cartilage, like a large trumpet, which hangs between his teeth, and serves him for hands: by one blow with his trunk he will kill a camel or a horse, and will raise a prodigious weight with it. His teeth are the ivory so well known in Europe, some of which have been seen as large as a man's thigh, and a fathom in length. Wild elephants are taken with the help of a female ready for the male: she is confined to a narrow place, round which pits are dug; and these being covered with a little earth scattered over hurdles, the male elephant easily falls into the snare. In copulation the female receives the male lying upon her back; and such is his pudicity, that he never covers the female so long as anyone appears in sight.

Yet Johnson's *Dictionary* represents more, far more, than mere quaintness and charm. Its publication represented a pivotal moment in the history of the English language; the only more significant moment was to commence almost exactly a century later.

Samuel Johnson had been thinking about and planning the structure of his dictionary for many years. He had been doing so in part to create a reputation for himself. He was a schoolteacher turned scribbler, known only in limited metropolitan circles as the parliamentary sketch-writer for the *Gentleman's Magazine*. He was eager to be better regarded. But he began the process also in response to these calls from the giants, these demands that something needed to be done.

Theirs was a near universal complaint. Addison, Pope, Defoe, Dryden, Swift, the *corps d'élite* of English literature, had each spoken out, calling for the need to *fix* a language. By that – *fixing* has been a term of lexicographical jargon ever since – they meant establishing the limits of the language, creating an inventory of its word-stock, forging its cosmology, *deciding exactly what the language was*. Their considered view of the nature of English was splendidly autocratic: the tongue, they insisted, had by the turn of the seventeenth century become sufficiently refined and sufficiently pure that it could only now remain static, or else henceforward deteriorate.

By and large they agreed with the beliefs of the Forty Immortals across the Channel (though loath they were to admit it): a national standard language needed to be defined, to be measured, to be laid down, chased in silver and carved in stone. Alterations to it could then be permitted or not, according to the mood of the great and the good, a home-grown forty, a national language authority.

Swift was the fiercest advocate of all. He once wrote to the Earl of Oxford to express his outrage that words like *bamboozle*, *uppish* and, of all things, *couldn't* were appearing in print. He wanted strict rules established banning such words as offensive to good sense. In future he wanted all spellings fixed – a firm orthography, the correctness of writing. He wanted the pronunciations laid down – with equally firm orthoepy, the correctness of speech. Rules, rules, rules: they were essential, demanded Gulliver's creator.

The language should be accorded the same dignity and respect as those other standards that science was at that time also defining. Physicists were wondering, what is blue, or yellow? How hot is boiling water? How long is a yard? How should what musicians knew as 'middle C' be defined? What, indeed, of the longitude of a ship? Enormous efforts were being made in this particular field at just the same time as the debate over the national language: a Board of Longitude had been set up by the government, funds were being disbursed, prizes offered, just so that a clock could be invented that would go to sea on a ship and be only almost imperceptibly inaccurate. Longitude was vitally important: so great a trading nation as Britain needed to have her ships' masters know exactly where they were.

And so, the thinking of great literary men went – if longitude was important, if the defining of colour and length and mass and sound was vital, why was the same import not given to the national tongue? As one pamphleteer wailed, appropriately, 'We have neither Grammar nor Dictionary, neither Chart nor Compass, to guide us through the wide sea of Words.'

No dictionary had proved adequate so far, said Swift and his friends: but, given the heights of perfection that the language had now achieved, one was now needed, and a dedicated genius must be found and be applied to the task of making one. It would accomplish two desirable deeds: the fixing of the language, and the maintenance of its purity.

Samuel Johnson could not have disagreed more. At least, he wanted to have no truck with ordering the language to remain pure. He might have liked it to – but he knew it couldn't be done. As to whether he thought it possible or desirable to fix it – theses have tumbled by the score from academic presses in recent years, arguing variously that Johnson did want to, or that he did not. The consensus now is that he originally planned to make a fix on the tongue, but, when he was halfway through his six-year task, he came to realize it was both impossible and undesirable.

One of his predecessors, Benjamin Martin, explained why: 'No language as depending on arbitrary use and custom can ever be permanently the same, but will always be in a mutable and fluctuating state; and what is deem'd polite and elegant in one age, may be accounted uncouth and barbarous in another.' This dictum, which appeared in a preface to still another half-baked attempt at a proper dictionary just a year before Johnson brought out his own, might as well have guided the Great Cham through his entire construction.

For all the heady talk among London's intelligentsia, it was actually the free market that prompted Johnson to begin. In 1746 a group of five London booksellers (the famous Messrs Longman among them) were seized with the idea that a brand-new dictionary would sell like hot cakes. They approached their favourite parliamentary writer, whom they knew to be both eager and broke, and made him an offer he could scarcely refuse: fifteen hundred guineas, half of it up front. Johnson agreed readily, with the sole caveat that he would seek as patron the man who was currently the arbiter of all that was good and worth while in literary England, Philip Dormer Stanhope, the fourth Earl of Chesterfield.

Lord Chesterfield was one of the most remarkable figures in the land: an ambassador, a lord-lieutenant of Ireland, a friend to Pope, Swift, Voltaire and Gay. It was Chesterfield who had forced England to adopt the Gregorian calendar, and it was Chesterfield whose letters to his bastard son Philip, advising him on his behaviour, became, when published, an indispensable vade-mecum of good manners. His imprimatur on the *Dictionary* would be valuable, his patronage of the project invaluable.

That he promised the imprimatur, but declined the patronage (except for handing to Johnson a draft for a measly ten pounds) and then went on to claim a part in Johnson's subsequent triumph became a source of well-publicized hard feelings. Lord Chesterfield, Johnson was to say later, taught 'the morals of a whore and the manners of a dancing-master'. Chesterfield had the elephantine hide of a true aristocrat and brushed off the criticisms as good-natured, which they were not.

His early advocacy of the *Dictionary*, plus the seven hundred and fifty guineas that the booksellers had placed in Johnson's hand, none the less set the 37-year-old editor to work. He took rooms off Fleet Street, hired six serving men as amanuenses (five of them Scotsmen, which would come as some comfort to James Murray, who was from Hawick) and settled down to the six years of unremitting drudgery that were to prove necessary. He had decided, as Murray was to decide a century later, that the best way – indeed the only way – to compile a full dictionary was to read: to go through all literature, and list the words that appeared on hundreds of thousands of pages.

It is an axiom that you have three overlapping choices in making a word-list. You may record words that are heard. You may copy the words from other existing dictionaries. Or you may read, after which, in the most painstaking way, you record all the words you have read, sort them, and make them into a list.

Johnson dismissed the first idea as far too cumbersome to be useful; he naturally agreed to the second – all lexicographers use earlier dictionaries as a foundation, to make sure they miss nothing; and, most significantly, he decided on the primary importance of the third choice, reading. Hence the taking of the rooms off Fleet Street, hence the buying or borrowing of books by the ton and the yard and the sack, and hence the hiring of the six men. The team of seven had been created to browse and graze through all existing writings, and to make a catalogue of all that was swept into the team's collective maw.

It was swiftly realized that it would be impossible to look through everything, and so Johnson imposed limits. The language, he decided, had probably reached its peak with the writings of Shakespeare, Bacon and Spenser, and so there was precious little need to look further back than their lifetimes. He ruled, therefore, that the works of Sir Philip Sidney, who was only thirty-two when he died in 1586, would usefully mark the starting-point for his search; and the last books published by newly dead authors would mark the end.

His *Dictionary* would thus be the result of a concerted trawl through just a century and a half of writing, with the odd piece of Chaucer thrown in for good measure. So Johnson took down these books and read, underlined and circled words he wanted, and annotated the pages he had chosen; he demanded that his men copy on to slips of paper the full sentences that displayed his chosen words; and these he then filed, to use when necessary, to illustrate the point he was making, the meaning of the word that he was trying to show.

And it was all those quoted meanings, a demonstration of the multiplicity of subtle shadings of sense that can be encompassed by the simple arrangement of a group of letters, that proved the great triumph of Johnson's *Dictionary*. For while we might laugh at the quaint charm of his definition of *elephant*, or of *oats* ('A grain which in England is generally given to horses, but in Scotland supports the people'), or *lexicographer* ('a writer of dictionaries; a harmless drudge, that busies himself in tracing the original, and detailing the signification of words'), we can only be staggered by his dealing with, say, the verb *take*. Johnson listed, with supportive quotations, no fewer than 113 senses of this particular verb's transitive form, and 21 of the intransitive. To seize, grasp or capture; to catch with a hook; to catch someone in an error; to win popular favour; to be effective; to claim to do something; to assume the right . . . to mount a horse, to flee, to perform what one does in removing one's clothing.

The list is almost endless: it was a mark of Johnson's genius that, armed with references from 150 years of English writings, he was able, essentially single-handedly, to find and note almost every use of every word of the day. Not simply *take*, but other common coin like *set*, and *do*, and *go* and hundreds upon hundreds of others. Small wonder that once his project was well under way, and the trifling business of his creditors' needs arose, he once barred the door to the milkman with his bed, crying from behind the door, 'Depend on it, I will defend this little citadel to the utmost!'

He finished amassing his list of the English word-stock in 1750. He spent the next four years editing the citations and choosing the 118,000 illustrative quotations (sometimes by the heresy of changing quotes he didn't like). Finally he completed the definitions of what were to become the 43,500 chosen headwords. He wrote some of these definitions from scratch, or else he borrowed substantial passages for others from writers he admired (as with *elephant*, which was partly the work of a man named Calmet).

He did not publish the completed work until 1755, however: he wanted to persuade Oxford University to grant him a degree, believing that if he was able to add it to his name on the title-page, it would do Oxford, the book's sale and himself – and not necessarily in that order – a lot of good. Oxford agreed; and on 15 April 1755 there appeared

A Dictionary of the English Language, in which the Words are deduced from their Originals; and Illustrated in their Different Significations, by Examples from the Best Writers to which are prefixed a History of the Language and an English Grammar, by Samuel Johnson, M.A., in Two Volumes.

The book, which went into four editions during Johnson's lifetime, was to remain the standard work, an unrivalled repository of the English language for the next century. It was an enormous commercial success, and was almost universally praised – particularly by the egregious Lord Chesterfield, who hinted that he had had rather more to do with the book's making than he had. This enraged Johnson; not only did he mutter about whores and dancing-masters, but he had up his sleeve the unkindest cut: under the definition of *patron* – which is what he had hoped Chesterfield might be – he had written 'a wretch who supports with indolence, and is paid with flattery'. But the noble Lord brushed this aside too.

There were some critics. The fact that Johnson allowed his own personality to invade the pages may today seem pleasant whimsy, but to some who wanted the book to be supremely authoritative, it was irritatingly unprofessional. Many writers sniped at the limited authority of some of those whom Johnson quoted – a criticism that Johnson himself anticipated in his preface. Some found the definitions patchy – some trite, some unnecessarily complicated (as with *network*: any thing reticulated, or decussated, at equal distances, with interstices between the intersections). A century after publication Macauley was to damn Johnson as 'a wretched etymologist'.

But, Macauley aside, many of the critics were probably just jealous, envious that Johnson had done what none of them could ever do. 'Any schoolmaster might have done what Johnson did,' wrote one. 'His *Dictionary* is merely a glossary to his own barbarous works.' But the writer was anonymous, and quite probably a disappointed rival. Or else a rabid Whig: Johnson was a noted Tory, and wrote with what some thought a distinctive Tory bias. So the book was merely 'a vehicle for Jacobite and high-flying tracts', wrote one Whig, doubtless a die-hard. One woman even disparaged Johnson for failing to include obscenities. 'No, Madam, I hope I have not daubed my fingers,' he replied archly. 'I find, however, that you have been looking for them.'

Yet the accolades were many. Voltaire proposed that the French model a new dictionary of their own on Johnson's; and the venerable Accademia della Crusca wrote from Florence that Johnson's work will be 'a perpetual Monument of Fame to the Author, an Honour to his own Country in particular, and a general Benefit to the republic of Letters throughout all Europe'. 'In an age of dictionaries of all kinds,' wrote a modern critic, 'Johnson's contribution was simply *primus inter pares*.' And Robert Burchfield, who edited the four-volume supplement to the *Oxford English Dictionary* in the 1970s, had no doubts. Johnson managed to be both a lexicographer and a supremely literate man: 'In the whole tradition of the English language and literature the *only* dictionary compiled by a writer of the first rank is that of Dr Johnson.'

Throughout it all, under the rains of slings, arrows, plaudits and encomiums, Johnson remained calmly modest. Not unduly so; for he was proud of his work, but awed by the magnificence of the language he, with such foolhardiness, had chosen to tackle. The book remained his monument. James Murray was to say in later years that whenever someone used the phrase 'the Dictionary', as one might say 'the Bible' or 'the Prayer-Book', he referred to the work by Dr Johnson.

But no, literature's Great Cham would have said that it was the words that were the truest monument and, even more profoundly, the very entities that those words defined. 'I am not yet so lost in lexicography,' he said in his famous preface, 'as to forget that words are the daughters of earth, and that things are the sons of heaven.' His life had been devoted to the gathering in of those daughters; but it was heaven that had ordained their creation.

Chapter Five

The Big Dictionary Conceived

---

elephant ('ɛlɪfənt). Forms: *α*. 4–6 oli-, olyfaunte, (4 *pl*. olifaunᴈ, faunтᴣ), 4 olyfont, -funt, 5–6 olifant(e, 4 olephaunte, 5–6 olyphaunt, 4–7 oli-, olyphant(e. *β*. 4 elifans, 4–5 ele-, elyphaunt(e, 5 elefaunte, 6 eliphant, 5–6 elephante, 6– elephant. [ME. *olifaunt*, a. OF. *olifant*, repr. a popular L. **olifantu-m* (whence Pr. *olifan*; cf. MDu. *olfant*, Bret. *olifant*, Welsh *oliffant*, Corn. *oliphans*, which may be all from ME. or OFr.), corrupt form of L. *elephantum, elephantem* (nom. *elephantus, -phas, phans*), ad. and a Gr. ἐλέφας (gen. ἐλέφαντος). The refashioning of the word after Lat. seems to have taken place earlier in Eng. than in Fr., the Fr. forms with *el-* being cited only from 15th c.

Of the ultimate etymology nothing is really known. As the Gr. word is found (though only in sense 'ivory') in Homer and Hesiod, it seems unlikely that it can be, as some have supposed, of Indian origin. The resemblance in sound to Heb. *eleph* 'ox' has given rise to a suggestion of derivation from some Phœnician or Punic compound of that word; others have conjectured that the word may be African. See Yule *Hobson-Jobson* Suppl., s.v. For the possible relation to this word of the Teut. and Slavonic name for 'camel', see OLFEND. The origin of the corrupt Romantic forms with *ol-* is unknown, but they may be compared with L. *oleum, olĭva*, ad. Gr. ἔλαιον, ἐλαία.]

1. a. A huge quadruped of the Pachydermate order, having long curving ivory tusks, and a prehensile trunk or proboscis. Of several species once distributed over the world, including Britain, only two now exist, the African and Indian; the former is the largest of extant land animals, and the latter is often used as a beast of burden, and in war.

The achievements of the great dictionary-makers of England's seventeenth and eighteenth centuries were prodigious indeed. Their learning was unrivalled, their scholarship sheer genius, their contribution to literary history profound. All this is undeniable –

and yet, cruel though it seems, who now really remembers their dictionaries, and who today makes use of all that they achieved?

The question begs an inescapably poignant truth, of the kind that dims so many other pioneering achievements in fields that extend beyond and are quite unrelated to this. The reality, as seen from today's perspective, is simply this: however distinguished the lexicographical works of Thomas Elyot, Robert Cawdrey, Henry Cockeram and Nathaniel Bailey, and however masterly and pivotal the creation of the Great Cham himself, their achievements seem nowadays to have been only stepping-stones, and their magnificent volumes very little more than curios, to be traded, hoarded and forgotten.

And the reason for this is principally that in 1857, just over a century after the publication of the first edition of Johnson's *Dictionary*, there came a formal proposal for the making of a brand new work of truly stellar ambition, a lexicographical project that would be of far, far greater breadth and complexity than anything attempted before.

It had as its goal a quite elegantly simple impertinence: while Johnson had presented a selection of the language – and an enormous selection at that, brilliantly fashioned – this new project would present *all of it*: every word, every nuance, every shading of meaning and spelling and pronunciation, every twist of etymology, every possible illustrative citation from every English author.

It was referred to simply as the Big Dictionary. When conceived it was a project of almost unimaginable boldness and foolhardiness, requiring great bravura, risking great nemesis. Yet there were men in Victorian England who were properly bold and foolhardy, who were more than up to the risks implicit: this was, after all, a time of great men, of great vision, of great achievement. Perhaps no time in modern history was more suited to the launch of a project of such grandiosity; which is perhaps why duly, and ponderously, it got under way. Grave problems and seemingly intractable crises threatened more than once to wreck it. Rows and delays surrounded it. But eventually, and by which time many of those great and complicated men who first had the vision were long in their graves, the goal, the goal of which Johnson himself might have dreamed, was duly attained.

And while Samuel Johnson and his team had taken six years to create their triumph, those involved in making what was to be, and still is, the ultimate English dictionary, took seventy years, almost to the day.

The Big Dictionary's making all began with the speech at the London Library, on Guy Fawkes' Day 1857.

Richard Chenevix Trench was officially designated by his contemporary obituarists as 'a divine'. The term is rarely used today, but it embraced all manner of good and eminent Victorians who pursued all kinds of callings, and who wore the cloth while doing so. At the time of his death in 1886 Trench was still regarded as more divine than anything else – he had had a glittering ecclesiastical career that culminated in his being made Dean of Westminster and then Archbishop of Dublin. He also was lame because of breaking both his knees: not because of any excess of piety, however, but because he fell down a gangplank while crossing on the boat to Ireland.

His topic on that lexicographically famous evening was intriguing: the theme, advertised in posters and flyers posted around west London, was 'On Some Deficiencies in Our English Dictionaries'. By today's standards the title seems self-effacing; but, given the imperial temper of the time, and the firm belief that English was the quintessential imperial language and any books that dealt with it were important tools for the maintenance of the Empire, the title offered an amply understandable hint of the impact that Dr Trench would be likely to have had.

He identified seven principal ways in which the dictionaries then available were to be found wanting – most of them were technical, and should not concern us here. But his underlying theme was profoundly simple: it was an essential credo for any future dictionary-maker, he said, to realize that a dictionary was simply 'an inventory of the language'. It was decidedly not a guide to proper usage. Its assembler had no business selecting words for inclusion, on the basis of whether they were good or bad. Yet all of the craft's earlier practitioners, Samuel Johnson included, had been guilty of doing just that. The lexicographer, Trench pointed out, was 'an historian . . . not a critic'. It was not in the remit of one dictator – 'or *Forty*' he added, with a cheeky nod at Paris – to determine what words should be used, and what should not. A dictionary should be a record of *all* words that enjoy any recognized life span in the standard language.

And the heart of such a dictionary, he went on, should be the history of each of the life spans of each of the words. Some words are ancient, and exist still; others are new, and vanish like mayflies. There are words that emerge in one lifetime, continue to exist through the next and the next, and look set fair to endure for ever; and there are those that deserve a less optimistic prognosis. Yet all of these types of word are valid parts of the English language, no matter that they are old and obsolete, or new and with questionable futures. Consider the golden question, said Trench: if someone needs to look up any word, then it should be there – for if not, then the work of reference that book purports to be becomes a nonsense, something to which one cannot refer.

Now he was warming to his theme: to chart the life of each word, he continued, to offer its *biography*, as it were, it is important to know just when the word was born, to have a record of the register of its birth. Not in the sense of when it was first spoken, of course – that, until the advent of the tape-recorder, could never be known – but when it was first written down. Any dictionary that was to be based on the historical principles that, Trench insisted, were the only truly valid principles, had to have, for every word, a passage quoted from literature that showed where each word was first used.

And after that, and for each word also, there should be sentences that show the twists and turns of meanings – the way almost every word slips in its silvery, fish-like way, weaving this way and that, adding subtleties of nuance to itself, and then perhaps shedding them as the public mood dictates. 'A Dictionary,' Trench said, 'is an historical monument, the history of a nation contemplated from one point of view, and the wrong ways into which a language has wandered . . . may be nearly as instructive as the right ones.'

Johnson's *Dictionary* may have been among the pioneers in presenting quotations (an Italian, for example, claimed his diction-ary had already done so in 1598) – but they were there only to illustrate *meaning*. The new venture that Trench seemed now to be proposing would demonstrate not merely meaning, but the history of meaning, the life-story of each word. And that would mean the reading of everything, and the quoting of everything that showed anything of the history of the words that were to be cited. The task would be gigantic, monumental and – according to the conventional thinking of the times – impossible.

Except that here Trench presented an idea – an idea that, to those ranks of conservative and frock-coated men who sat silently in the Library on that dank and foggy evening, was potentially dangerous, and even revolutionary. But it was the idea that in the end made the whole venture possible.

The undertaking of the scheme, he said, was beyond the ability of any one man. To peruse all of English literature – and to comb the London and New York newspapers, and the most literate of the magazines and journals – must be instead 'the combined action of many'. It would be necessary to recruit a team – moreover, a huge team, one probably comprising hundreds and hundreds of unpaid amateurs, all of them working *as volunteers*.

The audience murmured with surprise. Such an idea, obvious though it may sound today, had never been put forward before.

But then, some members said as the meeting was breaking up, it did have some real merit. It had a rough, rather democratic appeal to it. It was an idea consonant with Trench's underlying thought, that any grand new dictionary ought to be itself a democratic product, a book that demonstrated the primacy of individual freedoms, of the idea that one could use words freely, as one liked, without hard and fast rules of lexical conduct.

Any such dictionary certainly should not be an absolutist, autocratic product, such as the French had in mind: the English, who had raised eccentricity and ill-organization to a high art, and placed the scatterbrain on a pedestal, loathed such Middle European things as rules and conventions and dictatorships. They abhorred the idea of diktats – about the language, for heaven's sake – emanating from some secretive body of unaccountable immortals. Yes, nodded a number of members of the Philological Society, as they gathered up their astrakhan coats and white silk scarves and top-hats that night and strolled out into the yellowish November fog: Dean Trench's notion of calling for volunteers was a good one, a worthy and really rather noble idea.

And it was also, as it happens, an idea that would eventually permit the involvement in the project of one scholarly but troubled lexicographer *manqué*: Assistant Surgeon (Ret'd), United States Army, the Brevet Captain William Chester Minor.

This, however, was only the idea. It took twenty-two more years of sporadic and sometimes desultory activity before the new dictionary truly got off the ground. The Philological Society had already complicated matters: six months before Trench's famous speech it had set up an Unregistered Words Committee, had corralled along with Trench the boisterous Frederick Furnivall and Herbert Coleridge, the poet's grandson, to run it, and had planned to devote its corporate efforts to publishing a supplement dictionary of everything not found in those books that had already been published.

It took many months for the enthusiasm behind that project to abate – though it was given a nudge by the swift realization that so many words were being uncovered in searches that any supplement would be far, far bigger than any book, even Johnson's, that was already available. Once that was behind them, the Society formally accepted the idea of a wholly new dictionary: 7 January 1858, when the plan was adopted, is normally reckoned the starting-point, at least on paper.

Furnivall then issued a circular, calling for volunteer readers. They could select from which period of history they would like to read books – from 1250 to 1526, the year of the New English Testament, from then to 1674, the year when Milton died, or from 1674 to what was then the present day. Each of the periods, it was felt, represented the existence of different trends in the language's development.

The volunteers' duties were simple enough, if onerous. They would write in to the Society offering their services in reading certain books; they would be asked to read and make word-lists of all that they read, and would then be asked to look, super-specifically, for certain words that currently interested the Diction-ary team. Each volunteer would take a slip of paper, write at its top-left hand side the target word, and below, also on the left, details of the work cited: these were, in order, the date, author, title of the book or paper, volume and page number. Below that would appear the full sentence that illustrated the use of the target word. The technique has been employed by lexicographers up to the present day.

Herbert Coleridge became the first editor of what was to be called the *New English Dictionary on Historical Principles*. He undertook as his first task what may seem prosaic in the extreme: the design of a small stack of oak-board pigeon-holes, nine holes wide and six high, which could accommodate the anticipated 60,000 to 100,000 slips of paper that would come in from the volunteers. He estimated that the first volume of the Dictionary would be available to the world within two years. 'And were it not for the dilatoriness of many contributors,' he wrote, clearly in a tetchy mood, 'I should not hesitate to name an earlier period.'

Everything about these forecasts was magnificently wrong. In the end more than *six million* slips of paper came in from the volunteers; and Coleridge's dreamy estimate that it might take two years to have the first saleable section of the Dictionary on the streets – for it was to be sold in parts, to help keep revenues coming in – was wrong by a factor of ten. It was this kind of woeful and naïve underestimate – of work, of time, of money – that at first so hindered the Dictionary's advance. No one had a clue of what they were up against: they were marching blindfolded through molasses.

And Herbert Coleridge's early death slowed matters down even more. He died after only two years at work, at the age of thirty-one, and not even halfway through looking at the quotations of words beginning with 'A'. He had been caught in the rain on the way to a Philological Society lecture, and sat through it, in the unheated upstairs room in St James's Square, caught a chill and died. His last recorded words were: 'I must begin Sanskrit tomorrow.'

Furnivall took over, and threw all of his breezy energy and bovine determination into his work – but in the same madcap, irresponsible manner that had already made him a multitude of enemies. He had the bright and enduring idea of hiring a team of assistants, whom he would interpose between the volunteer-readers, now gaily sending in their slips of paper with the necessary quotations, and the editor himself.

The assistants could check the incoming slips for accuracy and value, then sort them into bundles and place them in the pigeon-holes. It would then be up to the editor to decide on the word he was going to 'do' – take out from its place in the alphabetically arranged pigeon-holes the bundle of quotations for that target word, and decide which of the quotations best suited his needs. Which one was the earliest was vitally important, of course; as were the others, thereafter, that demonstrated the slow progress of the word, as its meaning varied over the centuries, up to whatever was its primary meaning now.

But Furnivall presided over a project that, in spite all of his energies and enthusiasm, started slowly but clearly to die. For some reason, never quite explained, Furnivall had not the ginger to keep the hundreds of volunteers enthused, and so they, slowly and steadily, simply stopped reading, stopped sending in the slips. It seemed to many an insurmountable task. Many in fact sent back their books and the papers that Furnivall had sent to them to read – in 1879 alone they had returned two tons of *matériel*. The Dictionary was well and truly stalled, perhaps a victim of its own massive ambition. Furnivall's reports to the Society became shorter and shorter; his sculling expeditions, with waitresses from the ABC, longer and longer. In 1868 the *Athenaeum*, the journal that most closely followed the progress of the work, told its London readers that 'the general belief is, the project will not be carried out'.

But it did not die. James Murray, it will be remembered, had been a member of the Philological Society since 1869. He had already made a name for himself with publications on Scottish dialect, with huge editing tasks (of Scottish poetry) and with noble but unfinished projects (such as a planned work on the declension of German nouns). He had left the Chartered Bank of India, and resumed his beloved teaching, this time at the distinguished London public school Mill Hill.

Furnivall – a man who, though clearly committed to the Dictionary, simply lacked the personal qualities necessary to lead it – thought Murray a perfect choice as editor. He approached Murray, and others of the Society too: would not this astonishing young man (Murray was then just over forty) be the ideal candidate? And moreover, would not the Oxford University Press, with its academic distinction and comparatively deep pockets and its flexible view of literary time, be the ideal house to publish the work?

Murray was persuaded to produce some specimen pages, suggestions of how the work might look. He chose the words *arrow*, *carouse*, *castle* and *persuade*, and in the late autumn of 1877 the pages were duly sent off to Oxford, to the Press's notoriously difficult Delegates – essentially, the Board of Directors, who were renowned for being dauntingly highbrow, irritatingly pedantic and fiscally mean. Furnivall continued to meet other publishers and printers – the house of Macmillan was at one time deeply involved, but had a row with Furnivall and backed out – and made endlessly certain that the Big Dictionary remained on everybody's mind.

The twin notions, of selecting the right editor and the proper publisher, continued to vex the lexicographical and commercial literary establishments of England for the final years of the seventies. Oxford's Delegates first dismayed everyone by saying that they cared little for Murray's specimens: they wanted more proof that Murray had looked hard enough and fully enough for quotations for his four chosen words; they said they didn't like the way he had offered the words' pronunciations; and they dithered about whether his etymological section should be omitted (not least because they were already publishing a quite separate and scholarly *Etymological Dictionary* of their own).

In exasperation Murray and Furnivall looked hopefully towards the Cambridge University Press, but the Syndics there (the equivalent of Oxford Delegates) offered only a brusque rebuff. Lobbying went on in common rooms and London clubs for week after week. And as time passed, so Oxford became slowly persuaded that changes could be made, that the powers that be might ultimately find the pages of the proposed book to be acceptable, that Murray might well be the man, and that the Big Dictionary could in fact one day have the commercial and intellectual appeal that Oxford wanted.

It was finally on 26 April 1878 that Murray was invited up to Oxford for the first meeting with the Delegates themselves. He had come expecting to be terrified of them; they imagined they would be dismissive of him. But to everyone's surprised delight, he found that he rather liked the grand old men who sat in that great Oxford boardroom and, more to the point, they discovered in short order that they very much liked him. The upshot of the meeting was the Delegates' decision – in a moment of subdued and characteristically Oxonian jubilation, celebrated with a glass or two of bad dry sherry – to proceed.

Arguments over the details of contract – which were often bitter, but were rarely conducted in person by a decidedly other-worldly Murray (though his hard-headed wife Ada did have things to say) – took another full year. Finally, on 1 March 1879, almost a quarter of a century after the speech by Richard Chenevix Trench, a document was formally agreed upon: Murray was to edit, on behalf of the Philological Society of London, the *New English Dictionary on Historical Principles*, which would spread itself across an estimated 7,000 pages quarto, in four thick volumes, and take ten years to complete. It was still a woeful underestimate: but the work was now beginning properly, and this time it was never to stop.

Within days Murray had made two decisions. First, he would build a corrugated-iron shed in the grounds of Mill Hill School, he would call it the Scriptorium, and would edit the Dictionary from there. And second, he would write and have published a four-page appeal – 'to the English-speaking and English-reading public' – for a vast fresh corps of volunteers. The Committee, he declared, would 'want help from readers in Great Britain, America and the British Colonies, to finish the volunteer work so enthusiastically commenced twenty years ago, by reading and extracting the books which still remain unexamined'. The four sheets of paper – eight pages of writing – went out to the magazines and newspapers of the day, who regarded them as a press release and published such parts as seemed likely to interest their readers. They also went out to bookshops and news-stands, and assistants handed them to customers. Librarians gave them out as bookmarks, and there were small wooden cases in shops and libraries where the public could take them and read them at will. Before long they had found wide circulation all around the kingdom and her various dominions, old and new.

And some time in the early 1880s one copy, at least, left inside a book, or slipped between the pages of a learned journal, found its way to one of two large cells on the top floor of Block 2 of the Broadmoor Asylum for the Criminally Insane in Crowthorne, Berkshire. It was read voraciously by William Minor, a man for whom books, with which one of his two cells was lined from floor to ceiling, had become a second life.

Minor had now been an inmate at Broadmoor for eight years. He was deluded, true; but he was a sensitive and intelligent man, a graduate of Yale, and was well read and curious. He was, understandably, preternaturally anxious to have something useful to do, something that might occupy the weeks and months and years and decades – 'until Her Majesty's Pleasure be known' – that stretched without limit before him.

The invitation from a Dr James Murray of Mill Hill, Middlesex, NW, it seemed, promised an opportunity for intellectual stimulus, and perhaps even a measure of personal redemption, that was far better than any he could otherwise imagine. He would write immediately.

He took down paper and a pen, and in a firm hand wrote his address: *Broadmoor, Crowthorne, Berks*. A perfectly ordinary address. To anyone who did not know any better it was merely a means of describing an ordinary house, in an ordinary village, in a prettily rural royal county just beyond the boundaries of London.

And even if someone outside did know the word *asylum*, the sole definition that was available at the time was quite innocent in its explanation. The meaning was to be found in Johnson's *Dictionary*, naturally: 'A place out of which he that has fled to it, may not be taken.' An *asylum* was to Dr Johnson no more than a sanctuary, a refuge. William Chester Minor was quite content to be seen to write from inside such a place – just so long as no one looked too closely for the deeper and more sinister meaning that the word was gathering to itself in the hard times of Victorian England.

Chapter Six

The Scholar in Cell Block 2

---

bedlam ('bɛdləm). Forms: 1–3 **betleem**, 3 **beþ-þleæm**, 3–6 **beth(e)leem**, 4 **bedlccm**, 4–8 **bethlem**, 6– **-lehem**, 3–7 **bedlem**, 5 **bedelem**, 6 **bedleme**, 6–7 **-lame**, 6– **bedlam**. [ME. *Bedlem* = *Bethlem*, *Bethlehem*; applied to the Hospital of St. Mary of Bethlehem, in London, founded as a priory in 1247, with the special duty of receiving and entertaining the bishop of St. Mary of Bethlehem, and the canons, etc. of this, the mother church, as often as they might come to England. In 1330 it is mentioned as 'an hospital', and in 1402 as a hospital for lunatics (Timbs); in 1346 it was received under the protection of the city of London, and on the Dissolution of the Monasteries, it was granted to the mayor and citizens, and in 1547 incorporated as a royal foundation for the reception of lunatics. Thence the modern sense, of which instances appear early in 16th c.] . . .

2. The Hospital of St. Mary of Bethlehem, used as an asylum for the reception and cure of mentally deranged persons; originally situated in Bishopsgate, in 1676 rebuilt near London Wall, and in 1815 transferred to Lambeth. *Jack* or *Tom o' Bedlam*: a madman.

3. By extension: A lunatic asylum, a madhouse.

'Minor, William Chester. A thin, pale and sharp-featured man with light sandy-coloured hair, deep-set eyes and prominent cheek bones. He is thirty-eight years old, of superior education, indeed a surgeon, but of no known religion. He weighs ten stone, one pound, and is formally classified as being Dangerous to Others. He was charged with the willful murder of one George Merrett of Lambeth, was found Not Guilty on the Grounds of Insanity. He says he has been the victim of persecution for years – the victim of the lower classes, in whom he has no faith. Persons unknown are trying to injure him, with poison.'

So begin the case notes for Broadmoor Patient Number 742, based on an examination conducted in the afternoon of the day he was admitted, Wednesday, 17 April 1872.

Guards had brought him there in shackles, along with another murderer – a man who was classified as too insane to be tried – named Edmund Dainty: both had been waiting in gaol at Newington in Surrey until the necessary papers had been brought down from London. They were brought first by steam train to the small red-brick and Gothic railway station that had been built by and then named for Wellington College, one of the great public schools of southern England, which stood near by. A black Broadmoor landau, its roof closed shut, then took Minor and his escorts through the narrow, leafy lanes winding around the tiny village. The horses were sweating slightly as they hauled the four-wheel vehicle and its occupants up the low sandstone hill at the top of which stands Broadmoor itself.

The Special Hospital, as it is called today, still looks a forbidding place, even though much of what must have rendered it quite terrifying in Victorian times is now hidden discreetly behind its high, smoothly round-topped modern high-security walls. In 1872 Minor came to the original front gate: two triple-storeyed towers with heavily barred windows, with a high archway between, topped by a large black-faced clock. The arch was closed by a massive pair of thick green outer wooden doors. A peep-hole in one snapped open at the sound of the horses' hoofs, the doors swung back to reveal another set of heavy gates ten yards deeper into the asylum.

The landau moved swiftly inside, the front doors were slammed closed and bolted hard, and the lights in the dim and cavernous reception area were turned on. Minor was ordered to step out, to be searched. His chains were removed, and would be taken back to Surrey. The escorting tipstaff handed over the papers – a long warrant in elegant copperplate, under the signature of Henry Austin Bruce, Her Majesty's Principal Secretary of State for the Home Department. The asylum superintendent, a kindly and sympathetic man named William Orange, had his deputy sign the receipt.

Minor was led through the second set of gates and into Block 4, the admissions block. He heard the horses turn around, heard his escort get back on to the leather seat and order the driver to return to the railway station. He heard the outer gates open to let the carriage out, and close again. There was a resounding second crash as the inner metal gates shut and were bolted and chained. He was now formally and properly a Broadmoor inmate, confined in what would probably be his home for the rest of his natural life.

It was a fairly new home, however. Broadmoor had been opened just nine years. It had been built because the state's main lunatic asylum, the Hospital of St Mary of Bethlehem – from which we gain the word *bedlam*, a madhouse, and which was, by coincidence in Lambeth, less than a mile from the murder site – was now full to bursting. Legal recognition of criminal madness had been established by Parliament in 1800, and judges had for the past half century been dispatching into asylums, and sentencing to stay there until the monarch's 'Pleasure be known', scores of men and women who hitherto would have been sent to ordinary prisons.

The Victorians, with their characteristic mix of severity and enlightenment, believed the inmates could be kept securely away from the public to whom they were so dangerous, as well as properly treated. But the enlightenment only went so far: while nowadays the Broadmoor inmates are patients, and Broadmoor itself a special hospital, a century ago there was no mincing of words: the inmates were lunatics and criminals, they were treated by alienists and mad-doctors, and Broadmoor was indubitably an asylum in which they were firmly imprisoned.

Broadmoor certainly looked and felt – and was meant to look and feel – like a prison. It had been designed by a military architect,

Sir Joshua Jebb, who had previously created two of England's darkest high-security penitentiaries, Pentonville and Dartmoor. It had long, gaunt cell blocks, severe and intimidating; all the buildings were of dark red brick, all windows were barred, there was a huge wall with iron spikes and broken glass.

The institution slouched crab-like, ugly and forbidding, on top of its hill: villagers would look up towards it, and shudder. They tested the escape sirens every Monday morning: the banshee wails that echoed and re-echoed across the hills were spine-chilling; people said the birds remained silent, frightened, for many minutes afterwards.

But Minor, an American murderer – where to put him? The normal practice, which, to judge from his case notes, was almost certainly followed in Minor's case, was to spend several early days asking the newcomer about himself, and then, if he wanted to discuss it, about the crime that had caused him to be sent there. (One newcomer, asked about why he had killed his wife and children, told the superintendent: 'I don't know why I am telling you all of this. It's none of your business. As a matter of fact it was none of the judge's business either. It was *a purely family affair.*')

Once that was duly accomplished – and it was standard Broadmoor procedure never to ask again about the crime – the superintendent decided which of the six male blocks (there were two others for women, securely fenced off from the men) was most suitable. If the patient was judged suicidal (and his records thereafter being written on pink cards, not white) he was put in a cell in Block 6, where there were extra staff for observing him all the time; if he was diagnosed epileptic he was put in another cell in the same block, a special room that had padded walls and a wedge-shaped pillow so he could not suffocate himself during a fit.

If he was thought to be dangerous and violent he was also shut up in Block 6, or maybe the slightly less staffed Block 1 – the two blocks being known variously as the Strong Blocks, the Disturbed Blocks or, more recently, the Refractory Blocks. The two buildings, more grim and gaunt than the rest, were known by the inmates as the Back Blocks, because they had no view over the landscape. They were secure, tough, miserable.

After the first few days of interrogation the Broadmoor doctors realized that their new charge − who was a doctor himself, after all − was not epileptic, or liable to kill himself, or sufficiently violent to do anyone an injury. So he was sent to Block 2 − a relatively comfortable wing that was usually kept for parole patients. It was called 'the swell block', the word not so much used in the American sense as in the British, meaning it tended to be occupied by swells. A visitor once wrote that Block 2 had an atmosphere 'described by someone familiar with both, as identical with that at the Athenaeum Club'. It is difficult to imagine that too many of the members of this most genteel of London's gentlemen's clubs, and which included on its rolls most of the bishops and learned men of the land, were thrilled by the comparison.

Yet he was made more than just tolerably comfortable − not least because he was a well-born, well-educated man, and with an income: all the Broadmoor officials knew he was a retired soldier, with a regular army pension paid from the United States. So he was given not one cell but two, a pair of connecting rooms at the south end of the block's top floor. The rooms were kept unlocked by day; at night they were bolted from the outside. A long narrow vertical slot, too narrow for an arm to reach out, was used to observe the patient and his room: the design was such that an attendant could see everything within.

The windows had iron bars on the inside, but to compensate there was an enchanting view: a long shallow valley of cattle-filled meadows with the cows standing in the shadow of great oak trees, the Broadmoor tennis courts and small cricket pitch to one side, a line of low blue hills crowned with beeches in the distance. On that early spring day, with clear skies and lilacs and apple blossom and the songs of larks and thrushes, the sentence cannot have seemed altogether a nightmare.

At the north end of the corridor sat the guard – known at the asylum as the attendant – who kept watch over the twenty men on his floor. He had keys, and presided over the ever locked door to the floor itself, and would let them in and out of their rooms to visit the bathroom; and during the day he kept a small gas flame burning beside him, from a brass jet. The men were not allowed matches: this is where they came to light their cigarettes or their pipes, from the ration they were handed each week. (The tobacco all came from HM Customs service: anything confiscated as contraband at the ports was handed over to the Home Office, for distribution at the prisons and the state lunatic asylums.)

Within days the American Vice-Consul-General was writing, making sure that their hapless army officer was being well looked after. Might it be possible for 'our poor friend', he prayed, to have some of his personal effects sent down? (They had been left at the consulate to help pay any of the diplomats' expenses at court.) Is it in theory possible to visit? To cheer him up, could we send him a pound of Dennis's coffee, and some French plums? Mr Orange was silent on the specific matter of plums, but told the diplomat that Dr Minor could have whatever he liked, so long as it didn't prejudice his safety or the disciplined running of the asylum.

So a week later the official sent up a leather portmanteau by rail: it held a frock coat and three waistcoats, three pairs of drawers and four undervests, four shirts, four collars, six pocket handkerchiefs, a prayer-book, a box of photographs, four pipes, cigarette papers, a bag of tobacco, a map of London, a diary, and a fob-watch and gold chain – the last a family heirloom, it had been said during the trial.

Most important of all, the superintendent reported later, the doctor was given back his drawing materials: a deal drawing-box and contents, a paintbox and a collection of pens, a drawing-board, sketch-books and painting-cards. He would now be able to occupy his time constructively, which all patients were encouraged to do.

Over the succeeding months Minor furnished his cells comfortably – much, indeed, as a member of the Athenaeum might. He had money: a pension of about twelve hundred dollars a year was paid to his brother Alfred in Connecticut – he acted for William, whom the state had designated 'an incapable person' – and Alfred regularly telegraphed funds to England to keep his sick brother's running account up to date. Using this constant credit, Minor satiated his one consuming passion: books.

He demanded first that his own books be sent over from home in New Haven. Once they were installed he ordered, from the big London bookstores, scores upon scores of new and second-hand volumes, which he first stood in precarious piles in his cells until he asked – and paid for – bookshelves to be built. In the end he had converted the more westerly of the two rooms into a library, with a writing-desk, a couple of chairs and teak bookshelves that ran from floor to ceiling.

He kept his easel and paints in the other, easterly room; he also kept a small selection of wine and some bourbon with which the envoy kept him supplied. He took up the flute again, and gave lessons to some of his neighbour inmates. He also found he was permitted – and was well able to afford – to pay one of his fellow patients to perform work for him – tidying his room, sorting his books, cleaning up after a painting session. Life, which in those first months had been at least tolerable, now started to become really quite agreeable: Minor was able to live a life of total leisure and security, he was warm and reasonably well fed, his health was attended to, he could stroll along the long gravel pathway known as the Terrace, he could take his ease on one of the benches by the lawn and gaze at the shrubberies, or he could read and paint to his heart's content.

His cells still exist – not much at Broadmoor has changed in a century, and although Block 2 is now called Berkshire House, it is still much the preferred home for those patients who are in for the long haul. Economy and the exigencies of today's criminal justice and mental health systems mean that two patients are now housed where once there was only one: each of Minor's two rooms, the more westerly one that had been his library, the other that had been his sitting-room, offer home and hearth and some spartan comfort to a present-day inmate.

Minor's sanity, or lack thereof, was never in doubt. He was never so ill as to be ordered away from the benign atmosphere of Block 2 and into the harsher regime of the Back Blocks (though a strange and terrible incident in 1902 did take him away from his rooms for many weeks). But the ward notes show that his delusions became over the years ever more fixed, ever more bizarre, and that there seemed no likelihood that he would ever regain his reasoning. He was comfortable in Broadmoor, maybe; but there was nowhere else he could be allowed to live.

The ward notes from his first ten years show the sad and relentless progress of his downward spiral. Already at the time he was admitted he had a detailed awareness of the curious happenings that plagued him at night – always at night. Small boys, he believed, were put up in the rafters above his bed; they came down when he was fast asleep, chloroformed him and then forced him to perform indecent acts – though whether with them as boys, or whether with the women of whom he dreamed constantly, the record-keepers were never clear. He would awaken with abrasions around his nose and mouth where they had clamped the gas bottle; the bottoms of his pyjama legs were always damp, he said, indicating he had been forced to walk in a stupor through the night.

April 1873: 'Dr Minor is thin and anaemic, excitable in manner, though appears rational by day and occupies himself with painting and playing the flute. But at night he barricades the door of his room with furniture, and connects the handle of the door with the furniture using a piece of string, so that he will awaken if anyone tries to enter the bedroom.'

June 1875: 'The doctor is convinced that intruders manage to get in – from under the floor, or through the windows – and that they pour poison into his mouth through a funnel: he now insists on being weighed each morning to see if the poison has made him heavier.'

August 1875: 'The expression of his face in the morning is often haggard and wild, as though he did not obtain much rest. He complains that he feels as if a cold iron has been pressed against his teeth at night, and that something is being pumped into him. Otherwise, no change.'

A year later the demons were seeming to have a depressing influence. In February 1876 the doctors noted: 'A fellow patient stated today that Dr Minor came to see him in the Boot Room and said he would give him everything, if only he would cut his – Dr Minor's throat. An attendant was ordered to look after him.'

The following year was no better. 'Socially,' he was reported as explaining to an attendant in May 1877, 'all systems are based on schemes of corruption and knavery, and he is the subject of their machinations. This lies at the heart of the brutal torture to which he is subjected each night. His spinal marrow is pierced and his heart is operated on with instruments of torture. His assailants come through the floor.'

In 1878 technology becomes a part of the villainy. 'Electric currents from unseen sources are passed through his body, he insists. Electric buttons are placed in his forehead, he is placed in a wagon and trundled across the countryside.' He was taken as far afield as Constantinople, he told an attendant once, where he was made to perform lewd acts, in public. 'They are,' he declared, 'trying to make a pimp of me!'

But while the delusions clearly persisted and worsened over those early asylum years, the clinical notes do show – and crucially to this story – the parallel development of a more thoughtful and scholarly side to the afflicted man. 'With the exception of his impressions on the subject of his night-time visitations,' says one entry in the late 1870s, 'he talks very coherently and intelligently on most topics. He works in his bit of garden, and is fairly cheerful just now – but he has his days of moodiness and reserve.' A year later a doctor recorded simply: 'He is rational and intelligent for the most part.'

He also begins to settle down, and starts to regard the great hospital as his home, and the attendants as his family. 'He is not particularly aware that he is anxious to go back to America, as at one time he was,' wrote another doctor. 'All he asks is a little bit more freedom, perhaps to go and see sights in London, or perhaps visit the orchid show for which he had just received a card.' Yet the doctor who conducted this particular interview was certain of his patient's condition, and inscribed a sentence that seems in hindsight almost to have sealed Minor's eternal fate: 'There can be no doubt that Dr Minor, though on occasion very calm and collected, is generally speaking more abundantly insane, and shows himself to be more so, than he was some years ago. He has the calm and firm conviction that he is almost nightly the victim of torment and purposive annoyance, on the parts of the attendants and others connected with an infernal criminal scheme.'

It was at about this time that there came two developments, one of which by chance led indirectly to the other. The first stemmed from a factor that is not uncommon among those who commit appalling crimes: Minor became truly remorseful for what he had done, and made a resolution to try and make some kind of amends. It was with this in mind that he took the bold step of writing to his victim's widow, via the American Embassy, which he knew had helped to raise a fund for her back in the months immediately following the tragedy.

He explained to Eliza Merrett how inexplicably sorry he was for what he had done, and offered to try to help her in any way he could – perhaps by settling money on her or her children. Already Minor's stepmother, Judith, had contributed: now, perhaps, and if she would only be so gracious as to accept, he could do rather more.

The letter seems to have worked a small miracle: not only did Eliza agree to accept financial help from Minor, she also asked if it might be possible to visit him. It was an unprecedented request, that an incarcerated murderer be allowed to spend time with a relation of his victim; but the Home Office, after discussing the matter with Dr Orange, the Broadmoor superintendent, agreed to one experimental supervised visit. Accordingly, some time during late 1879 Eliza travelled up from Lambeth to Broadmoor, and first met the man who had ended her husband's life seven years before, and who had so drastically changed her own life, and those of her seven children.

The meeting, according to Dr Orange's notes, was at first tense, but it progressed well, and by its end Eliza had agreed to come again. Before long she was making monthly ventures down to Crowthorne, eager to talk with interested sympathy to this now seemingly harmless American. And though the conversations stopped short of developing into any real friendship, it is believed she made Minor an offer that was to lead to the second of the major developments of this period of his life. She apparently agreed to bring parcels of books to Minor from the antiquarian dealers up in London.

Eliza knew very little of books – indeed, she was barely literate. But when she saw how keenly Minor collected and cherished his old volumes, and when she listened to his querulous remarks about the delays and costs of the postal service between London and Crowthorne, she made an offer to collect his orders for him, and bring them down on her visits. And so it happened that month by month Eliza began delivering packages, wrapped in brown paper and sealed with twine and wax, from West London's great book emporiums, like Maggs and Bernard Quaritch and Hatchards.

The delivery system, such as it was, probably remained in place for only a few months – Eliza eventually took to drink, and lost all interest in the curious old man. But it appears to have been the most serendipitous event in Minor's otherwise melancholy life.

For it was in the early 1880s that he might have stumbled across the first of James Murray's famous appeals for volunteers, which asked for interested parties to indicate that they would be prepared to work on the new Dictionary. Murray first published his appeal in April 1879, and had 2,000 copies printed and circulated by booksellers: one would almost certainly have found its way, probably fairly soon after its distribution, into one or more of the packages that Eliza brought to Minor at the asylum.

The eight pages explained in very broad terms what was likely to be required. First there were Murray's own suggestions for the kind of books that needed to be read:

In the Early English period up to the invention of Printing so much has been done and is doing that little outside help is needed. But few of the earliest printed books – those of Caxton and his successors – have yet been read, and any one who has the opportunity and time to read one or more of these, either in the originals, or accurate reprints, will confer valuable assistance by so doing. The later sixteenth-century literature is very fairly done; yet here several books remain to be read. The seventeenth century, with so many more writers, naturally shows still more unexplored territory. The nineteenth-century books, being within the reach of everyone, have been read widely; but a large number remain unrepresented, not only of those published during the last ten years while the Dictionary has been in abeyance, but also of earlier date. But it is in the eighteenth century above all that help is urgently needed. The American scholars promised to get the eighteenth-century literature taken up in the United States, a promise which they appear not to have to any extent fulfilled, and we must now appeal to English readers to share the task, for nearly the whole of that century's books, with the exception of Burke's works, have still to be gone through.

After this, Murray listed rather more than 200 specific authors whose works, in his view, were essential reading. The list was quite awesome: most of the volumes were rare, and likely to be in the hands of only a very few collectors. Some books, on the other hand, were already available at Murray's newly established

Dictionary Library at Mill Hill: they could be sent to readers who promised to do work on them. (And vouched to return them: when Furnivall had been editor he found that a number of disgruntled readers used the lending scheme as a means of swelling their own library collections, and neither sent in the requested quotation slips, nor ever returned the books.)

Minor wrote to Murray, formally volunteering his services as a reader. It is not wholly clear, though, just when this was − not clear exactly when Minor first started his legendary work. Murray recalled later that he had received Minor's letter 'very soon after I commenced the Dictionary'. No correspondence between the doctor and the Dictionary has been traced, however, until 1885 − which is hardly 'very soon'.

But one clue exists: there had been an article in the *Athenaeum* magazine in September 1879, suggesting that Americans might like to become more keenly involved: and it is quite probable that Minor, who is known to have subscribed to the magazine in Broadmoor, would have seen it. Based on this assumption, on Murray's recollections, and on the records of Minor's contributions that have been lately unearthed in the *OED* archives, it seems probable that his relationship with the Dictionary got under way in either 1880 or 1881.

But where did Murray think his correspondent was living, and what did he think he did? Murray told a correspondent that he remembered only that the first and subsequent letters from Minor had been addressed to the Dictionary office simply from *Broadmoor, Crowthorne, Berkshire*. Murray was too busy to ruminate on the matter, no matter how curiously familiar the address might have been. By the time he read the first letter he had already received about 800 similar letters in response to his appeal − he was being swamped by the success of his entreaty.

He replied to Minor with his characteristic courtesy, saying that, on the basis of his apparent qualifications, enthusiasm and interest, he should start reading immediately, going through any of the volumes he might already have, or else looking to the Dictionary office for copies of books he might require.

In due course, Murray continued, the doctor could expect to receive particular word requests – in the particular event that the Dictionary editors had trouble finding quotations for a specific word on their own. For the time being, however, Dr Minor and all the other early respondents, to whom the editor expressed his 'considerable gratitude', should just start reading, should start making word-lists and writing quotations in a careful, systematic but general way.

Two additional sheets of printed paper that Murray was enclosing with the letter, and which underlined a formal agreement that Minor had been officially welcomed as a volunteer reader, would offer any necessary further advice.

But through all of this, Murray explained some years later, 'I never gave a thought to who Minor might be. I thought he was either a practising medical man of literary tastes with a good deal of leisure, or perhaps a retired medical man or surgeon who had no other work.'

The truth about his new American correspondent was a great deal more strange than this detached, innocent and other-worldly Scotsman could have ever imagined.

Chapter Seven

Entering the Lists

---

catchword ('kætʃwɜːd). [f. CATCH- 3 b + WORD.]
    1. *Printing.* The first word of the following page inserted at the right-hand lower corner of each page of a book, below the last line. (Now rarely used.) Also in *Manuscripts.*
    2. A word so placed as to catch the eye or attention; *spec.* **a.** the word standing at the head of each article in a dictionary or the like . . .
    1879 *Directions to Readers for Dict.*, Put the word as a catchword at the upper corner of the slip. 1884 *Athenæum* 26 Jan. 124/2 The arranging of the slips collected . . . and the development of the various senses of every Catchword.

The two small closely printed sheets that came as an addendum to Murray's first letter turned out to be a set of meticulously worded instructions. When his morning mail was delivered by the ward staff that day, Minor must have fallen upon this one envelope eagerly, reading and rereading its contents. But it was not the content alone that fascinated him: a list of rules for Dictionary helpers was not the cause of his excitement.

It was the simple fact that they had been sent to him in the first place. The letter from James Murray must have represented, in Minor's view, a token of further forgiveness and understanding, which Eliza Merrett's visits to him had already suggested. The invitation seemed a long-sought membership badge of the society from which he had been so long estranged. By being sent these sheets of rules he was, he felt, being received back into a corner of the real world. A corner that, admittedly, was still housed in a pair of cells in an alien madhouse – but one that had firmly forged links to the world of learning, and connections with a more comfortable reality.

After a decade of languishing in the dark slough of imprisonment, intellectual isolation and remove, Minor felt that at last he was being hoisted back up on to the sunlit uplands of scholarship. And with what he saw as this re-enlistment in the ranks, so Minor's self-worth began, at least marginally, to re-emerge, to begin seeping back. From the little evidence that survives in his medical records, he appears to have started recovering his confidence and even his contentment, both with every moment that he spent reading Murray's acceptance letter, and then when he prepared to embark on his self-set task.

For a while at least he seemed truly happier. Even the sternly worded Victorian ward notes of the day hint that the temper of this usually suspicious, broody, prematurely elderly-looking middle-aged man (he was now coming up to his fiftieth birthday) had somehow started to turn. He was undergoing, even if only for a short while, a sea-change in his personality – and all because, at long last, he had something valuable to do.

Yet in its very value lay a problem, as Minor saw it. The doctor came swiftly to realize, and was daunted by the realization, that this great work's immense potential value to history, to posterity and to the English-speaking world meant it had to be done properly. Murray's papers had explained that the Dictionary was all about the gathering of *hundreds of thousands* of quotations. It was a task that was almost unimaginably vast. Could it be done from an asylum cell?

Minor was both wise enough to understand and to ask himself the question (since he knew well where he was, and why he was there) and then, in a partial answer, to applaud Murray for having taken the right approach to the work on which he was about to embark (his own love of books and literature giving him some knowledge of dictionaries, and an appreciation of what was good and what not so good about those that had already been published).

So on reflection he decided that he very much wanted to work for the project, and to be a part of it – not solely because it would give him something worth while to do – which was his first reason – but mainly because in his opinion Murray's plan for doing it was so self-evidently right.

But Murray's plan meant there was clearly going to be much more to his cell-bound duties than the mere enjoyment of a blissful and leisured romp through the history of published English literature. Minor needed now to pay absolutely scrupulous regard to what he read, to trawl religiously for whatever happened to be needed by Murray's team, and eventually to select from the cod of his net the very best possible entries to send away to be included in the book.

Murray's notes showed him how this might best be done. The quotations, said the editor's first page, were to be written on half-sheets of writing paper. The target word – the *catchword* as Murray liked to call it – was to be written at the top left. The crucial date of the quotation should be written just below it, then the name of the author and the cited book, volume, page number and, finally, the full text of the sentence being quoted. Some books that were important and well known and likely to be used a great deal would have pre-printed slips already – readers assigned to these books needed only to write to Mill Hill to have some sent; otherwise, Murray asked, please write out your own slips in full, arrange them alphabetically and send them on to the Scriptorium.

All this was simple enough. But, everyone wanted to ask, just what words were to be sought out?

Murray's early rules were clear and unambiguous: *every* word was a possible catchword. Volunteers should try to find a quotation for each and every word in a book. They should perhaps concentrate their efforts on words that struck them as rare, obsolete, old-fashioned, new, peculiar or used in a peculiar way; but also they should look assiduously for ordinary words as well, providing that the sentence that included it said something about the use or meaning of the word. Special attention needed to be paid to words that seemed to be new or tentative, obsolete or archaic, so that the date could be used to help fix the moment of their introduction into the language. All that, Murray hoped, was surely plain enough.

But then again, asked would-be readers – how many quotations should be supplied for each word? As many as convenient, Murray wrote back, especially where different contexts tended either to explain differences in the meaning, or helped to illustrate the subtle variations in a particular word's usage. The more quotation slips that came in to the iron shed he had built in Mill Hill, the better: he assured readers he had an ample supply of assistants to sort them, and that his floors had been especially strengthened to hold them.

(More than two tons of slips of papers had already come in from Coleridge's and Furnivall's first efforts, Murray added. But he didn't allow as to how many of them had been nibbled at by mice or ruined by damp, nor did he reveal that one lot was found in a baby's bassinet, and a load of slips beginning with the letter 'I' had been left in a broken-bottomed hamper in an empty vicarage, or that the entire letter 'F' had been accidentally sent off to Florence, and that thousands of slips were so poorly handwritten that, Murray reported to a friend, it would have made for easier reading if they had been written in Chinese.)

The second sheet of notes seemed to Minor to offer rather more practical, if much more prosaic, help. It first made clear that Murray had a fund from which he could repay the postage to those volunteers who sent packages of slips, but who could not afford to; and it asked that the packages be sent to Mill Hill by Book Post, with their ends unsealed, so that Murray didn't have to pay fines for those that had been shut with even the tiniest piece of the adhesive that Post Office regulations forbade.

Many early readers turned out to be dreadfully confused: they simply did not understand the scope of their allotted task. For example, asked a couple of them, did every single use of the word *the* within any one book require an illustrative quote? There would be tens of thousands from any volume, before any of the substantial words were even begun. And further, wailed one of the women readers, what if one had ploughed through all 750 pages of a volume, just as she had, and found not a single rare word to extract?

Murray's notes offer a tolerant and genial enough response to this kind of complaint, though a faint sense of his Calvinist asperity glimmers between the lines. No, he spoke through moderately gritted teeth, there was really no need to offer scores of illustrations for definite articles and prepositions, unless the circumstances turned out to be very strange. And no, no, no! Books were *not* to be scoured for rare words *alone* – he had to remind volunteers of this fact time and again. Readers must find and note all and any words that seemed interesting, or that were quoted in interesting and signifying ways, or in ways that were *good*, *apt* or *pithy*.

As an example of the dangers of the process so far, he said, he had received no fewer than fifty quotes for the word *abusion* (which means perversion of the truth), but had had only five for the much more common word *abuse*.

'My editors have to search for precious hours for quotations for examples of ordinary words, which readers disregarded, thinking them not worthy of including,' he wrote. Think simple, Murray kept insisting: think simple.

And then, half exasperated that he evidently still hadn't been clear enough, he laid down a distilled version of his instruction, a golden rule, a sentence that was to become the readers' epigraph. He wanted readers simply to be able to say: 'This is a capital quotation for, say, *heaven*, or *half*, or *hug*, or *handful*; it illustrates the meaning or use of the word; it is a suitable instance for the Dictionary.' Follow that kind of thinking, Murray insisted, and you will not go too far wrong.

Minor read and clearly understood all of this. He looked about his library-cell, scanning the volumes in the astonishing collection that he had already accumulated over the previous ten years. He took out the list of books that had come with Murray's original pamphlet. He would see first if he had any on his shelves that might in time prove useful.

All of a sudden his books, which had hitherto been merely a fond decoration and a means of letting his mind free itself from the grim routines of Broadmoor life, had become his most precious possession. For the time being at least he could set aside his imaginings about the harm that people were trying to inflict on him and his person: it was instead his hundreds of books that now needed to be kept safe, and away from the predators with which he believed the asylum to be infested. His books, and his work on the words he found in them, were about to become the defining feature of his newly chosen life. For the next twenty years he would do almost nothing at Broadmoor except enfold himself and his tortured brain in the world of his books, of their writings, and of their words.

He was maverick enough, originally minded enough, to see that he could do better than follow Murray's orders to the letter. Given his peculiar position, his leisure, his library, he could do more, do otherwise. It took him some days of pondering exactly how he might best serve the project; but after some weeks of thinking he came up with what he thought was the way to tackle the task. He made a decision. He took down from his shelves the first of his books, and laid it open flat on his desk.

We cannot be sure which book it was. For sake of illustration, though, let us say the first volume, and one which we know he had and used, was a leather-bound, gold-and-marble-edged translation of a French book called *Compleat Woman*, by one Jacques Du Bosc. It had been published in London in 1693. It had been translated by a man identified only as 'N. N.'

His arguments for starting with this in particular, and indeed for reading it at all, were many. It was a good, seventeenth-century work, it was obscure and exotic, it was filled no doubt with strange and amusing words. After all, Murray had exhorted his volunteers to examine this specific period of literary history. 'The seventeenth

century, with so many more writers, naturally shows still more
unexplored territory.' Du Bosc's book, in its anonymous translation, fitted the bill splendidly.

So Minor took from a drawer a single quire of white paper and
a bottle of black ink, and he selected a pen with the very finest
nib. He folded the paper so that it made a booklet, eight pages
thick. Then, with perhaps one last glance down from his cell
window at the lush countryside below, he settled in to read his
chosen book, line by line, paragraph by paragraph, with slow and
infinitely measured care. As he did so, he began a routine that he
had planned during his early days of preparation.

Each and every time he found a word that piqued his interest
he wrote it down, in tiny, almost microscopic letters, in its proper
position on the eight-page quire he had made.

The unique manner of his procedure was soon to become a
hallmark of Minor's astonishing accuracy and eye for detail. His
work would win the admiration and awe of all who were later to
see it; even today, the quires of paper preserved in the *OED*
archives are such as to make people gasp.

Let us choose as an example the moment when he came across
the word *buffoon*. He was first struck by the significance of
its appearance, in a suitably illustrative sentence, on Du Bosc's
page 34. He promptly wrote it down in his tiny, perfectly neat,
perfectly legible handwriting, on the first page of his blank booklet. He wrote it in the first column, and decided to place the
word and its page number in the column about a third of the way
down.

This placing was precise, and it was carefully chosen. The reason
for this was his certainty that sooner or later he would find another
interesting word beginning with the same letter *b*, that there was
a very good chance it would have to be put before *buffoon*, and
only a very much slimmer chance that it would need to be put
after (because with *buffoon*'s second letter being *u*, there were only
three possibilities – finding a further word whose second letter

was again *u*, or one with the only other legitimate second letters, *w* – with only one word, *bwana* – or *y*).

Sure enough, a few pages later he came across the interesting word *balk*, with a nice quotation, and so deserving to be entered in the quire. He placed it on the list above *buffoon*, but with enough space in the event that a *b* word came along that had a second letter somewhere in the alphabet between the new *a* and the old *u*. Five pages further on he then sighted with some pleasure the word *blab* – a word of the very kind he had anticipated – and so in it went too, levered into the space that he had so artfully retained below *balk* and well above *buffoon*.

And thus did the word-list for the first of Minor's cellful of books begin – word after word after word, each one with its spelling exact, its location in the quire perfectly appropriate, the page number where it was to be found in the source-book precise. From *atom* and *azure*, to *gust* and *hearten*, *fix* and *foresight*, the list went on and on. Some of the words occurred many times – *feel*, for example, which Minor recorded as cropping up on sixteen of Du Bosc's pages, although some of these turned out to be *feeling*, either the gerund (as in 'I can't help feeling this way') or the noun (as with 'the feeling of which you speak is painful').

It would have taken him many weeks, perhaps months, to complete this first word-list. Perhaps it was well into the year 1883 by the time he had finished it. But even though fully four years had now elapsed since Murray had sent out his first appeal pamphlet, and forty months since the first nudge to American readers in the *Athenaeum* magazine, and a year, maybe two, since Minor had read one or other of the appeals and had decided to become involved, he still had not sent one single quotation slip down to the Scriptorium. For all the staff of the Dictionary knew, he had lost interest, become overwhelmed, dropped out.

But that could not have been further from the truth. Minor in fact had quite another plan of attack – a working method that turned out to be very different from that of all other volunteer readers, but which soon marked him out as uniquely valuable in the making of the great Dictionary.

For once he had completed the monumental task of writing his first word-list from his first book, he replaced that volume and took down another. Perhaps his next was Francis Junius, *The Painting of the Ancients*, from 1638, or Thomas Wilson's *The Rule of Reason*, from 1551. Perhaps something quite different. It could have been any one of hundreds of books, for he had a prodigious collection, and it would be his practice to select one, then another, and then yet another, and write a new word-list for each one. One book might take him three months to complete, in the kind of detail he felt his distant editors would demand.

And so he would work away, day after day – the tiny spy-window in his door clicking open and shut every hour or so from the outside as the Broadmoor attendants checked on the safety and the existence of their strange patient. He would be working hard, deep in thought and in rapt concentration: he would index and collect and collate words and sentences from each of the books, until his prison desk was heavy with the quires of paper, each one containing a master-list of the indexed words from his eclectic, very valuable and much valued little gem of a library.

Although we cannot be sure which of his books he read first, we do know the titles of some of the books that he did read. Most of them, it turns out, reflect his keenly forlorn interest in travel and history. One can only imagine how his poor mind must have raced, trapped as it was in his book-lined retreat on the top floor of his cell block. How frustrated and pinioned he must have felt, reading line after line of such books as that by Thomas Herbert, written in 1634, and titled *A Relation of Some Yeares Travaile Begunne Anno 1626 into Afrique and the Greater Asia*; one can only suspect how homesick Minor must have felt for Trincomalee (and his native girls) on reading and indexing Nicholas Lichefild's 1582 translation of Lopes de Castanheda's *First Booke of the Historie of the Discoverie and Conquest of the East Indias*.

One by one, his collection of carefully assembled word leaflets mounted up. By the autumn of 1884 he had enough of them, a large enough selection of words for which he had readily accessible quotations, to begin inquiring of the Dictionary editors – and Murray himself in particular – which catchwords, precisely, were then needed. For while all the other volunteers would simply read their assigned books, note down interesting quotations on their slips of paper as they came across them and send them off in bundles, Minor, with all the time on his hands, was able to extrapolate on his radically different, home-grown approach.

With his rapidly growing collection of word-lists and his indexes, he stood ready now to help the Dictionary project as it needed to be helped, by sending over quotations at the precise time the editors needed them. He could keep up; he could be abreast of the progress of the Dictionary all the while, because he had ready access to the words that were needed, as and when they were wanted. He had made a key, a Victorian word-Rolodex, a diction-ary-within-a-dictionary, and instantly available. The quires of lists on his desk represented an accumulated creation of which he was quite rightly and jealously proud.

His practice was first to write to the Dictionary, and ask what letter or what word was being worked on. Then, on receiving a reply, he would refer to his own index-quires, to see if he had already noted down the wanted word. If he had – and, given his method, and his wide and energetic reading, it was more than likely that he had – he would follow his own notation of the page number or numbers, and go straight to the word's appearance or appearances in one of his books. Then, and only then, he would transcribe the best sentence containing the word on to a ready-made quotation-slip and send it directly to the Scriptorium.

It was an unprecedented approach – the kind of technique that only someone with an immense amount of energy and disposable time could contemplate. And of course it was a technique that suited the editors famously: they knew now that in all probability they had, 'on tap', as it were, and down at this mysteriously anonymous address in Crowthorne, a supply of fully indexed words, together with their associated citations and quotations.

With the arrival of Minor's first letter, saying what he had done and how ready he was for further inquiry, Murray's hard-pressed staff discovered that life had become in theory very much easier. From this moment forward they were not obliged only to ferret through their shelves and pigeon-holes, and to trawl through thousands of existing slips for quotations that might or might not exist for a word they wanted to include. They could simply decide on a word that was giving them problems, write to Crowthorne and ask for it.

With good fortune – and with a high statistical likelihood – they would in due course receive a letter and a package from Minor, giving the precise chapter and verse for whatever was wanted, enclosing the quotation slips at the very instant they were needed to be pasted on to a page for the compositors, the typesetters and the printers.

The first word to be tried in this way was a deceptively simple one (to the extent that any individual word is simple compared to any other). It was a word that was due to be included in the Dictionary's second fascicle, in preparation for publication in the late summer of 1885. Please inspect your word-lists, wrote an assistant, to see if you can find in them references to the word *art*, and to all its derived forms.

The letter went directly to Minor at Broadmoor, as his invitational letter had suggested. Whichever of Murray's assistants first asked him the question had no ideas about the man from whom an answer was sought. For many years hence no one in the Scriptorium was to learn anything about him, except for the undeniable truth that he was very good at his job, very quick, and on his way to becoming an indispensable member of the new Dictionary team.

Art was to be his first test.

Chapter Eight

Annulated, art, brick-tea, buckwheat

poor (puɑ(r), pɔə(r)), *a.* (*sb.*) Forms: α. 3–5 **pouere** (**povere**), 3–6 **pouer** (**pover**), (4 **poeucre, poeure, pouir**), 4–5 **poer, powere**, 5 **poyr**, 5–6 **power**, (6 **poware**). β. 3–5 **poure**, 4–6 **powre, pour**. γ. 3–7 (–9 *dial.*) **pore**, 4–7 **poore**, (6) 7– **poor**. δ. *Sc.* and *north. dial.* 4–6 **pur**, 4–8 **pure**, (4 **puyre**, 5 **pwyr, poyr**, 6 **peur(e, pwir, puire**), 6– **puir** (ü), (9 **peer**). [ME. *pov(e)re, pouere, poure*, a. OF. *povre, -ere, poure*, in mod.F. *pauvre*, dial. *paure, pouvre, poure=* Pr. *paubre, paure*, It. *povero*, Sp., Pg. *pobre*:–L. *pauper*, late L. also *pauper-us*, poor. The mod.Eng. *poor* and Sc. *puir* represent the ME. *pōre*: with mod. vulgar *pore*, cf. *whore* and the pronunciation of *door, floor*.

On account of the ambiguity of the letter *u* and its variant *v* before 1600, it is uncertain whether ME. *pouere, poure, pouer*, meant *pou-* or *pov-*. The phonetic series *paupere(m, paupre, paubre, pobre, povre*, shows that *povre* preceded *poure*, which may have been reached in late OF., and is the form in various mod.F. dialects. But the 15th and early 16th c. literary Fr. form was *povre*, artificially spelt in 15th c. *pauvre*, after L. *pauper*, and ME. *pōre* (the source of mod.Eng. *poor*) seems to have been reduced from *povre* like *o'er* from *over*, *lord* from *loverd*. Cf. also POORTITH, PORAIL, POVERTY. But some Eng. dialects now have *pour* (paur), which prob. represents ME. *pour* (puːr).]

I. 1. a. Having few, or no, material possessions; wanting means to procure the comforts, or the necessaries, of life; needy, indigent, destitute; *spec.* (esp. in legal use) so destitute as to be dependent upon gifts or allowances for subsistence. In common use expressing various degrees, from absolute want to straitened circumstances or limited means relatively to station, as 'a poor gentleman', 'a poor professional man, clergyman, scholar, clerk', etc. The opposite of *rich*, or *wealthy*. **poor people**, the poor as a class: often with connotation of humble rank or station . . .

6. Such, or so circumstanced, as to excite one's compassion or pity; unfortunate, hapless. Now chiefly *colloq.*

In many parts of England regularly said of the dead whom one knew; = late, deceased.

The first slips of snow-white unlined paper, six inches by four, and covered with Minor's neat and distinctively American hand-writing in greenish black ink, began to drift out from the Broad-moor post-room in the spring of 1885. By the late summer they were arriving at their destination in small brown-paper packets every month, and then larger packets every week. Before long the gentle shower of paper had turned into a raging blizzard, one that was to howl up from Crowthorne unceasingly for almost all of the next twenty years.

The paper slips were not, however, sent to Mill Hill. By the time Minor had begun to engage in the second stage of his work, contributing the quotations rather than amassing the lists, Murray and his team had all moved up to Oxford. The editor had been persuaded to give up his comfortable job as a schoolteacher, and, despite the poor pay and the interminable hours, he had taken the plunge into full-time lexicography.

This was in spite of a general mood of malaise and wretchedness. Murray's experiences with the first years of work on the Big Dictionary were far from happy, and many were the times he had vowed to resign. The Delegates at the Press seemed parsimonious and interfering; the pace of work was proving insufferably slow; his health was suffering from the interminable hours, his monoma-niacal devotion to an almost impossible task.

But then there was one sustaining fact: the first of the fascicles, the revenue-producing instalments into which Oxford insisted that the Dictionary be divided, had at last been published, on 29 January 1884.

Nearly five years had elapsed since Murray had been appointed editor. Twenty-seven years had passed since Richard Chenevix Trench had given his famous address in which he called for a new English dictionary. Now, in a muddy off-white cover and with its sheets half uncut, was the first part, 352 pages' worth of all the known English words from *a* to *ant*, published by the Clarendon Press, Oxford, at a price of twelve shillings and sixpence.

Here, at last, was the first morsel of substance: part one of the *New English Dictionary on Historical Principles, Founded Mainly on the Materials Collected by the Philological Society, edited by James A. H. Murray, LL.D., Sometime President of the Philological Society, with the Assistance of Many Scholars and Men of Science.*

Murray could not help but be proud; the problems that seemed so insuperable, and which so pressed down on him, would tend to vanish whenever he held the flimsy paper-covered volume in his hand. And in a sudden sunburst of birthday-eve optimism the editor – he would be forty-seven in less than a week declared that he now felt confident in predicting that the final part would be published in eleven years' time.

It was in fact to take another forty-four.

But now, after all the years of waiting, the interested world could at least see the magnificent complexity of the undertaking, the detail, the filigree work, the sheer intricacies of exactitude that the editors were bent on compiling. Those in England could write and receive a copy for twelve and six; those in America received a fascicle printed in Oxford, but published by Macmillan in New York, for three dollars and twenty-five cents.

The first part's first word – once the four pages devoted to the simple letter 'A' had been accounted for – was the obsolete noun *aa*, meaning a stream or watercourse. There was a quotation supporting its existence from a work of 1430, which had a reference to the still rather damp and water-girt Lincolnshire town of Saltfleetby, in which, four centuries before, there had been a rivulet known locally as '*le Seventowne Aa*'.

The first properly current word in the fascicle was *aal*, a Bengali or Hindi name for a plant related to the madder, from which a dye could be extracted and used to colour clothes. Andrew Ure's 1839 *Dictionary of Arts, Manufactures and Mines* provided the authority: 'He has obtained from the aal root a pale yellow substance which he calls morindin.'

And then the first properly English word – if, a linguist might quibble, there ever is such a thing. It was to be *aard-vark*, the half-armadillo, half-anteater that lives in sub-Saharan Africa and has a sticky two-foot tongue. Three quotations are offered, the earliest from 1833.

Thus does the vast emporium of words begin to display itself, through *acatalectic* and *adhesion*, via *agnate* and *allumine*, to *animal*, *answer* and, finally, to *ant*. By that last, Murray's team meant a great deal more than simply 'the small social insect of the Hymenopterous order'; there is also the contraction for *ain't*, a rare prefix meaning *anti-* as with *antacid* and more commonly the suffix appended to make words like *tenant*, *valiant*, *claimant* and *pleasant*. Three hundred and fifty pages of scholarly amassment, the first pages of what would in more than four decades' time swell to no fewer than 15,487.

It was in the new Scriptorium in Oxford that Murray was to do all future work on the Dictionary. He and Ada and their considerable family – they had nine children at this time – had moved there in the summer of 1884, six months after *A–Ant*. They had taken a large house on what were then the northern outskirts of the city, at 78 Banbury Road. It was called Sunny-side. The house, large and comfortable in the manner of north Oxford (a sedate settling-ground for the university's greater dons and lesser institutes), exists still, together with the red pillar-box that the Post Office erected outside to swallow up the immense amounts of outgoing letters. Today the house is occupied by a popular anthropologist, and he has changed it little enough on the outside.

Only the Scriptorium – the Scrippy, as the Murray family knew it (and Murray's own dictionary defines it as 'the room in a religious house set apart for the copying of manuscripts'), has gone. Perhaps not surprisingly: no one, even in Victorian times, much liked the iron and corrugated-tin construction, fifteen feet by fifty, that was put up in the back garden. The next-door neighbour said it spoiled his view, and so Murray had it sunk into a three-foot trench, which made it damp and cold for the staff, and produced a huge bank of discarded earth that offended the neighbours even more. When finished, people said it looked like a tool-house, a stable or a wash-house, and those who laboured in it cursed the monkish asceticism of its construction and its irredeemably bone-chilling cold, and called it 'a horrid, corrugated den'.

But it was twenty feet longer than the Mill Hill Scriptorium (which does still exist, an annexe to the library of what is still a costly and fashionable school), and the arrangements for filing, sorting and then using the incoming quotation slips – which by now were flooding in at the rate of more than a thousand each day – were much improved.

There were 1,029 pigeon-holes built at first (Coleridge had had just fifty-four); then banks of shelves were built as the volume and the sheer weight of slips became unmanageably large. Long and well-polished mahogany tables supported the texts selected for the word of the day or the hour, and large churchly lecterns held up the main dictionaries and reference books to which Murray and his workers made constant reference. The leader himself had placed his seat and desk on a dais back in the Mill Hill days; here at Oxford there was a more democratically level floor, but Murray's stool was taller than the rest, and he continued to preside from it with unchallenged authority, seeing all, missing little.

He organized the workings of the Scriptorium as might an officer on a battlefield. The slips were the peculiar province of the quartermaster, and Murray was a superb Q M G. The packages of slips would come in each morning. One reader would check quickly to see if the quotation was full, and all words were spelled properly; then a second – often one of Murray's children, each employed almost as soon as literate, paid sixpence a week for half an hour a day and rendered precociously crossword-capable – would sort the contents of each bundle into the catchwords' alphabetical order. A third worker would then divide the catch-words into their various recognized parts of speech – *bell* as noun, *bell* as adjective, *bell* as verb for instance – and then a fourth employee would see that the quotations assembled for each were arranged chronologically.

Then one of Murray's assistants would subdivide the meanings of each word into the various shades it had enjoyed over its lifetime; also at this point (and if he had not done so earlier) he would make a first stab at writing that most crucial feature of most dictionaries – the definition.

Defining words properly is a fine and peculiar craft. There are rules – a word (to take a noun as an example) must first be defined according to the class of things to which it belongs (mammal, quadruped), and then differentiated from other members of that class (bovine, female). There must be no words in the definition that are more complicated or less likely to be known than the word being defined. The definition must say what something is, and not what it is not. If there is a range of meanings of any one word – *cow* having a broad range of meanings, *cower* having essentially only one – then they must be stated. And all the words in the definition must be found elsewhere in the dictionary – a reader must never happen upon a word that he cannot discover elsewhere in the same book. Contrive to follow all these rules, and stir into the mix an ever pressing need for concision and elegance – and if the craftsman is true to his task a proper definition will probably result.

By now the words from the envelope of quotations would have been assembled into the smallest of subgroups, each with a stated meaning and a definition – either just written by a junior, or written some time before when the word was in a half-completed state. It remained now to divide these subgroups chronologically, so as to demonstrate – with the army of quotations – just how the shades of meaning of the catchword had altered and evolved over its life span.

Once this was done, Murray would take the collections of slips for each of the subgroups for any distinct and defined target word, and arrange or rearrange or further subdivide them as he saw fit. He would write and insert the word's etymology (which Oxford, despite its own etymological dictionary, did in the end see fit to allow Murray to include) and its pronunciation – a tricky decision, and one likely to provoke, as it has, ceaseless controversy – and then make a final selection of the very best quotations. Ideally there would be at least one sentence from the literature for each century in which the word was used – unless it was a very fast-changing word, and needed more quotations to suggest the speed of its new shadings.

Finally, with that all squared away, Murray would write the concise, scholarly, accurate and lovingly elegant definition for which the Dictionary is well known – and send the finished columns over to the Press. It would be set in a Clarendon or an Old Style typeface (or in Greek or other foreign or ancient English or Anglo-Saxon face when needed), and returned to the Scriptorium, printed in galley proofs. It was ready to be set on to a page, and the page made into a form for placing on the great letterpress engines in the stone printing works down the back of Walton Street.

Murray's letters tell a great deal about the difficulty of the task he had set himself – and that which the publishers, who wanted to see a return on their investment, in turn had set him. The expressed hope was that two parts – 600 pages of finished Dictionary – might be published each year. Murray himself tried gallantly to complete work on thirty-three words every day – and yet 'often a single word, like *Approve* . . . takes ¾ of a day itself'.

Murray spoke of the trials of the work in his presidential address to the Philological Society, and in a subsequent *Athenaeum* article in March 1884 – an article that led to his first real contact with Minor. He referred to the difficulty 'of pushing our way experimentally through an untrodden forest where no white man's ax has been before us'.

Only those who have made the experiment know the bewilderment with which editor or sub-editor, after he has apportioned the quotations for such a word as *above* . . . among 20, 30 or 40 groups, and furnished each of these with a provisional definition, spreads them out on a table or on the floor where he can obtain a general survey of the whole, and spends hour after hour in shifting them about like pieces on a chess-board, striving to find in the fragmentary evidence of an incomplete historical record, such a sequence of meanings as may form a logical chain of development. Sometimes the quest seems hopeless; recently, for example, the word *art* utterly baffled me for several days: something had to be done with it; something was done and put in type; but the renewed consideration of it in print, with the greater facility of reading and comparison which this afforded, led to the entire pulling to pieces and reconstruction of the edifice, extending to several columns of type.

It was about this time, when Murray was so very vexed over *art*, that one of his assistants – or perhaps it was Murray himself – wrote the first official request to Broadmoor. They wanted Minor to find out if he had earmarked any quotations for *art* that suggested other meanings, or which came from earlier dates, than had been assembled so far. Sixteen distinct shades of meaning had been uncovered for the noun: perhaps Dr Minor had some more, or some further illumination of the word. If so, then he – and anyone else, for that matter – should kindly send them back to Oxford, post-haste.

Eighteen letters duly came in about the word from a variety of readers who had seen the *Athenaeum* article. One of the replies, and undeniably the most fruitful, came from Broadmoor.

In comparison to all the other readers, who had offered merely a sentence or two, the unsung Dr Minor had enclosed no fewer than twenty-seven. He struck the workers in Oxford as not only a meticulous man but also very prolific, and able to tap deep into wells of knowledge and research. The Dictionary team had made a rare find.

It has to be said that most of Minor's quotations for this particular word came from a somewhat obvious source: Sir Joshua Reynolds's famous *Discourses*, written in 1769, the year after he became President of the Royal Academy. But they were of inestimable value to the Dictionary-makers – and as proof, standing there today as mute memorial to the beginnings of his work, is the first known quotation that William Chester Minor had placed in the finished book.

It is the first-but-one quotation under the sense *The Arts*, and it reads simply:

1769 SIR J. REYNOLDS *Disc.* i. Wks. 1870 I. 306. There is a general desire among our Nobility to be distinguished as lovers and judges of the Arts.

Unwittingly, Sir Joshua's words were to provide the starting-point for a relationship between Murray and Minor that would combine sublime scholarship, fierce tragedy, Victorian reserve, deep gratitude, a mutual respect and a slowly growing amity that could even be termed friendship, in the loosest sense. Whatever called, it was a link that would last the two men until death finally separated them thirty years later. The work that Minor did for the Dictionary, and that began with Reynolds's *Discourses*, continued for the next two decades; but some stronger bond than a simple love of words had also been forged, and it was one that kept these quite different elderly men connected intimately for half as long again.

It was to be seven years before they met, however. During that time Minor began to send out his quotations at a prodigious rate – at times many more than a hundred new slips every week, as many as twenty a day, all in his neat, firm hand. He would always write to Murray rather formally, straying only rarely into matters that were not within his self-appointed purview.

The first correspondence that survives, from October 1886, was largely about agricultural matters. Perhaps the doctor, taking a break from his work at the table, had stood up to stretch and had gazed wistfully from his cell window down at the farm labourers in the valley below, watching them stacking the late autumn sheaves and drinking warm cider under the oaks. He refers in his letter to a book he is reading called *Maison Rustique, or the Countrey Farme* (in an edition by Gervase Markham, published in 1616) and to occurrences of the verb *bell* – as when the ripening hops swell out in bell shapes in late August. *Blight* too catches his attention, as well as *blast*, and then *heckling*, which on farms once meant the process of separating the flax plant stem from stem, and only later became used in a political sense, to catechize someone, to make their arguments stand up to severe scrutiny, as a flax plant might stand when divided for the scutcher.

He liked the word *buckwheat* too – and finds such niceties as *ointment of buckwheat* and the French phrase *blé noir*. He clearly revels in his work: one can almost feel him squirming with teenage excitement as he offers 'I could give you more if you wanted', and as a teasing bonus throws in a small temptation on the thoroughly amusing word *horsebread*. He signs off, seeming to will a response from the great man on the great Outside: 'I trust same may be useful to you – Very truly yours, W. C. Minor, Broadmoor, Crowthorne, Berks.'.

The tone of this and other such letters as survive seems halfway between the obsequious and the detached, dignified and controlled on the one hand, and leavened with Uriah Heep-like toadying on the other. Minor wants desperately to know that he is being helpful. He wants to feel involved. He wants, but knows he can never demand, that praise be showered on him. He wants respectability, and he wants those in the asylum to know that he is special, different from the others in their cells.

Though he has no idea at all of his correspondent's character or circumstances – thinking him still 'a practising medical man of literary tastes with a good deal of leisure' – Murray seems to recognize something of his pleading tone. He notices, for instance, the curious way that Minor seems to prefer to be working on those words that were current – like *art* first, then *blast* and *buckwheat* – and that were in the process of being placed into the succession of pages, parts and volumes of the moment. Murray notes in a letter to a colleague that Minor clearly very much wanted to stay up to date – that unlike most other readers he had no interest in working on words that were destined for volumes and letters to be published years and decades hence. The editor writes later that he felt Minor clearly wanted to be able to feel involved, to enjoy the impression that he, Minor, was somehow a part of the team, doing things in tandem with the scribes up at the Scriptorium.

Minor was none too far from Oxford, after all – perhaps he felt as though he were at a detached college, like St Catherine's Society or Mansfield Hall, and that his cells – or what Murray still thought of as his comfortable, book-lined brown study – were just a rurally detached extension of the Scriptorium, a den of scholarly creation and lexical detective work. Had anyone chosen to ponder further, he might have wondered at the strange symmetry of the two men's settings – pinioned as each was among great stacks of books, single-mindedly devoted to learning of the most recondite kind, each man's only outlet his correspondence, in great daily storms of paper and floods of ink.

Except there was a difference: Minor remained profoundly and irreversibly mad.

The Broadmoor attendants had noticed some improvement in the very early 1880s, when he first replied to the appeal from Mill Hill. But as the years went on, and as Minor passed dejected and alone through the milestone of his fiftieth birthday in June 1884 – his elderly stepmother having visited him the month before, on her way home to America from Ceylon, where she had stayed since her husband's death – so the old ills returned, reinvigorated, reinforced.

'Dear Dr Orange,' he writes to the Broadmoor superintendent at the beginning of the next September, 'The defacement of my books still goes on. It is simply certain that someone besides myself has access to them, and abuses it.' His handwriting is shaky, uncertain. He heard his cell door opening at 3 a.m. the night before, he says, and goes on, raving, 'The sound of that door, as you may verify, since the alteration, is unmistakable; and you could be as morally sure of its closure by the sound, as of anything you do not really see.' If there is no other remedy, he warns, 'I shall have to send my books back to London, and have them sold.' Thankfully this small tantrum was short-lived. Had it continued, or worsened, the Dictionary might have lost one of its closest and most valuable friends.

A month later a new obsession grips him. 'Dear Dr Orange – Let me mention one fact that falls in with my hypothesis. So many fires have occurred in the US originating quite inexplicably in the interspace of ceiling and floor that, I learn now, Insurance Companies refuse to ensure large buildings – mills, factories – which have the usual hollow spacing under the floor. They insist upon solid floors. All this has come to notice within ten years; but no one suggests any explanation.'

Except Minor, that is. Fiends have been creeping about in the interstices between floors and ceilings, and have wrought mischief and committed crimes – not least in Broadmoor, where they hide and crawl out at night, to abuse the poor doctor nightly, mark his books, steal his flute and abuse him cruelly. The hospital, he says, must have solid floors built in: otherwise, no fire insurance, and a host of nightly misdeeds.

The daily reports flow in a kind of seamless syrup of insanity. Four cakes stolen; his flute gone; his books all marked; he himself frog-marched up and down the corridor by Attendants James and Annett. A spare key used at night to allow villagers into his rooms to abuse him and his possessions. Minor, in his drawers and shirt, stockings and slippers, complaining that small pieces of wood were forced into his lock, that electricity was used on his body, that 'a murderous lot' had beaten him during the night and had left a savage pain all along his left side. Scoundrels came to his room.

Attendant Coles came at 6 a.m. and 'used his body'. 'It is a very dirty business,' he screamed one morning, standing now only in his drawers, 'that a fellow cannot sleep without Coles coming in like that.' Again as before: 'He made a pimp of me!'

And yet as came the madness, so came the words. Many of those that fascinated him were Anglo-Indian, reflecting his birthplace: there was *bhang, brinjal, catamaran, cholera, chunam* and *cutcherry*. He liked *brick-tea*. By the time of the middle 1890s he became very active working on the letter 'D', and though there were some Hindustani words like *dubash* and *dubba* and *dhobi*, he was interested also in what were regarded as the core-words of the Dictionary – and contributions of quotations are in the *OED* archives for words like *delicately, directly, dirt, disquiet, drink, duty* and *dye*. He was able more often than not to supply the quotation for the first use of a word – always an occasion for celebration. For the use of the word *dirt* as meaning earth, he quotes from John Fryer's *New Account of East India and Persia*, published in 1698. For one meaning of *magnificent*, for one of *model*, for *reminiscence* and for *spalt*, the first work by Du Bosc also provided ideal material.

The Dictionary staff at Oxford noticed only one small and strange rhythm to Minor's frantic pace: that in the high summertime rather fewer packages would come. Perhaps, they speculated innocently, Dr Minor liked to spend the warm days outside, away from his books – a reasonable explanation indeed. But when the autumn came around, and the evenings began to darken, so he worked ceaselessly again, replying to every request, asking repeatedly and anxiously about the progress of the enterprise, and inundating the team with ever more packages of slips – more quotations, even, than were needed.

'One could wish that Dr Minor had made about half the number of references,' wrote Murray to another editor, overwhelmed, 'but indeed one never really knows what words will come of use till one comes to deal with the word lexicographically.'

His method of working was very different from everyone else's, in that he was sending in to Oxford only slips of quotations for words that he knew were actually wanted, and not all and any words that merely interested him, as most other volunteers did. For that reason it is more difficult to make a quantitative comparison, to set the numerical achievement of his work against that of the other great contributors. Perhaps at the end of the project he had actually sent in no more than 10,000 slips, which sounds a fairly modest number. But as virtually all of them proved to be useful, and because every one of them was wanted and had been ordered up, so his achievement as a contributor more than equals the effort achieved by some others, in sending 10,000 slips *a year*.

The Oxford team were indeed grateful. The preface to the first completed volume, *Volume I: A–B*, when finished in 1888 – a full nine years after the project was begun – contains a one-line mention. It might as well have been a page of fulsome thanks: and it made their contributor supremely proud, not least because it was, by happenstance, discreet enough to offer no hint to others of his strange situation. It said simply, and elegantly: 'Dr W. C. Minor'.

Grateful though they might have been, the Oxford team were also becoming, as time went on, very, very puzzled. And Murray was more puzzled than all of them.

Who exactly was this brilliant, strange, exacting man? they asked each other. Murray attempted, fruitlessly, to inquire. Crowthorne was less than forty miles from Oxford, an hour by the Great Western Railway via Reading. How was it that Minor, so distinguished and energetic a man, and so much a neighbour, was never to be seen? How could there be a man of such lexicographical skills, who had so much leisure and energy and lived so very close, and yet never seemed to want to see the temple to which he sent so many thousands of offerings? Where was the man's curiosity? What was his pleasure? Was he somehow unwell, disabled, frightened? Could it be that he felt intimidated by the company of great Oxford men like these?

The answer to the deepening mystery came about in a curious manner. It was delivered to Murray by a passing scholar-librarian, who stopped by at the Scriptorium in 1889 to talk about more serious matters. In the course of a talk that ranged across the entire spectrum of lexicography he made a chance reference to the Crowthorne doctor.

How kind the good James Murray had evidently been to him, remarked the scholar. 'How good you have been to our poor Dr Minor.'

There was a startled pause, and the assistants and secretaries in the Scriptorium who had overheard the conversation suddenly stopped in their tracks. As one, they looked up, towards where their leader and his visitor were sitting.

'*Poor* Dr Minor?' asked Murray, as perplexed as any of those who were now keenly listening. '*What can you possibly mean?*'

Chapter Nine

The Meeting of Minds

‖ **dénouement** (de'numã). [F. *dénouement,*
dénoûment, formerly *desnouement,* f. *dénouer, desnouer,*
in OF. *desnoer* to untie = Pr. *denozar,* It. *disnodare,* a
Romantic formation from L. *dis-* + *nodāre* to knot,
nodus knot.]

 Unravelling; *spec.* the final unravelling of the com-
plications of a plot in a drama, novel, etc.; the cata-
strophe; *transf.* the final solution or issue of a
complication, difficulty, or mystery.

Modern literary myth maintains, even today, that the strangest
puzzle surrounding William Chester Minor's career was this: just
why did he not attend the Great Dictionary Dinner – a dinner to
which he was invited, and that was held in Oxford on the glittering
evening of Tuesday, 12 October 1897?

It was Jubilee Year, and Oxford was in more than a mood for
a party. The Dictionary was at long last going well. The faltering
progress of the early years was now accelerating – the fascicle
Anta–Battening had been published in 1885, *Battentlie–Bozzom* in
1887, *Bra–Byzen* in 1888. A new spirit of efficiency had settled
on the Scriptorium. And as crowning glory Queen Victoria had
in 1896 'graciously agreed', as the court liked to say, that the just
completed third volume – embracing the entirety of the infuriating
letter 'C' – should be dedicated to her.

An aura of majestic permanence had all of a sudden invested
the Dictionary. There was no doubt now that it would eventually
be finished – for since it had been regally approved, who could
now ever brook its cancellation? With that happy realization,

and now that the Queen had done her part, so now Oxford, in high mood for celebration, decided it could follow suit. James Murray deserved to be given honours and thanks: and who more appropriate than the great man's adopted university to bestow them.

The university's new Vice-Chancellor decided that a big dinner – *slap-up*, to employ a phrase that the Dictionary was eventually to quote from 1823 – should be held in Murray's honour. It would be staged in the huge hall at The Queen's College, where by old tradition a scholar with a silver trumpet sounds a fanfare to summon guests in to dine. It would celebrate what *The Times*, on the day of the dinner, proclaimed to be 'the greatest effort probably which any university, it may be any printing press, has taken in hand since the invention of printing . . . It will not be the least of the glories of the University of Oxford to have completed this gigantic task.' The evening would be a memorable Oxford event.

As indeed it was. The long tables were splendidly decorated with flowers and with all the best silverware and crystal that Queen's could roust from its cellars. The menu was forthright and English – clear turtle soup, turbot with a lobster sauce, haunch of mutton, roast partridges, Queen Mab pudding, strawberry ice. Like the Dictionary itself, it was also flavoured generously, but not too generously, with a hint of Gallicisms: *sweetbreads after the mode of Villeroi, grenadines of veal, ramequins*. The wines were plentiful and excellent: an 1858 Amontillado, an 1882 Maraschino of Zara, a Château-d'Yquem and Champagne by Pfungst, 1889. The guests wore white tie, academic robes, medals. During the speeches – and after a Loyal Toast at which the graciousness of Her Majesty was loyally noted, and her six decades on the throne proudly congratulated – they smoked cigars.

They must have smoked long and well. There were no fewer than fourteen speeches – Murray on the entire history of Diction-ary-making, the head of the Oxford University Press on his belief that the project was a great duty to the nation, and the egregious

Furnivall, as lively and amusing as ever, taking time from recruiting buxom Amazons from the ABC tea-house to come a-rowing with him to speak on what he saw as Oxford's heartless attitude towards the admission of women.

Among the guests could be counted all the great and good of the academic land. The editors of the Dictionary, the Delegates of the Press, the printers, members of the Philological Society and, not least, some of the most assiduous and energetic of the staff and volunteers.

There was Mr F. T. Elworthy of Wellington, the Reverend W. E. Smith of Putney, Lord Aldenham (better known by friends of the Dictionary as Mr H. Hucks Gibbs), Mr Russell Martineau and Monsieur F. J. Amours. The list was long: and so sonorous were the names and so evidently awesome their achievements, the diners, well into their port and cognac by now, heard them out in a silence that was easy to confuse with rapture.

As it happens the most copious remarks that were made that night about the volunteers relate to two men who had much in common: both were Americans, both spent time in India, both were soldiers, both were mad; and, though both were invited, neither one of them came to the Oxford dinner.

The first was Dr Fitzedward Hall, who came from Troy, New York. His was a bizarre story. Just as he was going up to Harvard in 1848, his family demanded that he set off for Calcutta to track down an errant brother. His ship was wrecked in the Bay of Bengal; he survived and became fascinated by Sanskrit, studying it to the point where he was eventually offered the Chair in Sanskrit at Government College in what was then called Benares, the holiest city in the Ganges valley. He fought for the British side as a rifleman during the 1857 Mutiny, then left India in 1860 and became a professor of Sanskrit at King's College, London, and librarian at the India Office.

And then, quite precipitously, his life fell terribly apart. No one is sure why, except that he had a furious row with a fellow Sanskrit scholar named Theodor Goldstücker. It was a row of such gravity – linguists and philologists were known to be mercurial and hold eternal grudges – that it caused Hall to quit the India Office, have himself summarily suspended from the Philological Society and leave London for a small village in Suffolk.

People there said he was a drunkard, a foreign spy, hopelessly immoral and an academic phoney. He in turn accused all Britons of rounding on him, of ruining his life, of driving away his wife and displaying only a 'fiendish hatred' of Americans. He turned the key in the lock of his cottage in Marlesford and – except for the occasional steamer voyage back home to New York – lived the life of a near total country recluse.

And yet he wrote, every single day, to Murray at Oxford – a correspondence that continued for twenty years. The two men never met – but over the years Hall without complaint compiled slips, answered queries, offered advice, and remained the staunchest ally of the Dictionary during its bleakest days. Small wonder but that Murray wrote in the great preface: 'above all we have to record the inestimable collaboration of Dr Fitzedward Hall, whose voluntary labours have completed the literary and documentary history of numberless words, senses and idioms, and whose contributions are to be found on every page'.

Those at the dinner knew why he did not come: they knew he was a recluse, a hermit, that he was *difficult*. But no one knew – or so the story has long had it – exactly why the man next mentioned did not come. Murray, in writing the celebrated preface, had been almost equally generous in his praise: 'also the unflagging services of Dr W. C. Minor, which have week by week supplied additional quotations for the words actually preparing for press'. 'Second only to the contributions of Dr Fitzedward Hall,' Murray was to write a little later, 'in enhancing our illustration of the literary history of individual words, phrases and constructions, have been those of Dr W. C. Minor, received week by week.'

But where, asked the gathered assembly, was Dr Minor? He

was living only at Crowthorne, sixty minutes away by the green-and-gold steam trains of the Great Western. He was not notorious as an ill-tempered misanthrope, like Dr Hall. His letters had always been noted for their courtesy and solicitousness. So why could he not have the courtesy to come? To some who dined at Queen's on that glorious autumn evening, Dr Minor's absence must have seemed a melancholy footnote to an otherwise glorious literary moment.

The received wisdom has it that Murray was perplexed, even vaguely irritated. According to one version of the story, it is said that he vowed, with all the knowledge of his lexicography, to take a leaf from Francis Bacon, who in 1625 had written in English the axiom from the *hadith*, to the effect that 'If the hill will not come to Mahomet, Mahomet will go to the hill.'

It is said that he promptly wrote to Minor, his letter supposedly reading as follows:

You and I have now known each other through correspondence for fully seventeen years, and it is a sad fact that we have never met. Perhaps it has never proved convenient for you to travel; maybe it has been too expensive; but while it is difficult indeed for me to leave the work of the Scriptorium even for one day, I have long wanted to meet you, and may I perhaps suggest that I come to visit you. If this is convenient, perhaps you might suggest a day and a train, and if convenient for me I will telegraph the time of my expected arrival.

Minor wrote back promptly, saying that he would of course be delighted to receive the editor, that he was so sorry that physical circumstances – he did not elaborate – had made it hitherto impossible for him to come up to Oxford, and suggested a number of trains from those listed in the *Bradshaw*. Murray duly selected a November Wednesday, and a train that, with a change in Reading, was due in to the Wellington College Railway Station shortly after lunch.

He telegraphed the details to Crowthorne, wheeled out his

faithful black Humber tricycle and, with his white beard blowing over his shoulder in the chilly breeze, set out down the Banbury Road, past the Randolph Hotel, the Ashmolean and Worcester College, and to the 'up' platform of Oxford Station.

The journey took just a little over an hour. He was pleasantly surprised, on arriving at Crowthorne, to find a brougham and a liveried coachman waiting for him. His long-held assumption that Minor must be a leisured man of letters was reinforced: perhaps, he thought to himself, he was even a man of means.

The horses clip-clopped through the fog-damp lanes. The magnificent pile of Wellington College lay neatly in the distance, a respectable way from Crowthorne village itself, which was no more than a cluster of cottages, the piles of lawn-leaves smouldering behind them. It was a pretty little place, quiet, well wooded and rather self-contained.

After a couple of miles the coachman swung the horses into a poplar-lined driveway that climbed a long, low hill. The cottages thinned out, and were replaced by a number of smaller, red-brick houses of a rather more severe look. Then the horses stopped before an imposing front gate, a pair of towers with a great black-faced clock between, and a green-painted door that was being opened by a servant.

Murray removed his cap and unbuttoned the Inverness tweed cape that had protected him from the cold. The servant said nothing, but ushered him inside and up a flight of marble stairs. He was swept into a large room with a glowing coal fire and a wall covered with portraits of gaunt-looking men. There was a large director's desk and, behind it, a portly man of obvious importance. The servant backed out and closed the door.

Murray advanced towards the great man, who rose. Murray bowed stiffly, and extended his hand.

'I, Sir, am Dr James Murray of the London Philological Society,' he said in his finely modulated Scottish voice, 'and editor of the *New English Dictionary*.

'And you, sir, must be Dr William Minor. At long last. I am most deeply honoured to meet you.'

There was a pause. Then the other man replied: 'I regret not, sir. I cannot lay claim to that distinction. I am the Superintendent of the Broadmoor Asylum for the Criminally Insane. Dr Minor is an American, and he is one of our longest staying inmates. He committed a murder. He is quite insane.'

Murray, as the story then continues, was in turn astonished, amazed and yet filled with sympathetic interest. 'He begged to be taken to Dr Minor, and the meeting between the two men of learning who had corresponded for so long and who now met in such strange circumstances was an extremely impressive one.'

The story of this first meeting is, however, no more than an amusing and romantic fiction. It was created by an American journalist named Hayden Church, who lived in London for most of the first half of this century. It first appeared in England in the *Strand* magazine in September 1915, and then again, revised and amplified in the same journal, six months later.

In fact Church had already tried it out on an American audience, writing anonymously for the *Sunday Star* in Washington, DC, in July 1915. The story was splendidly sensationalized, with the kind of lurid multilayered headline that has sadly gone almost out of fashion: AMERICAN MURDERER HELPED WRITE OXFORD DICTIONARY read the first, extending over all eight columns of the page. MYSTERIOUS CONTRIBUTOR TO AN ENGLISH DICTIONARY PROVED TO BE A RICH AMERICAN SURGEON CONFINED IN BROADMOOR CRIMINAL LUNATIC ASYLUM FOR A MURDER COMMITTED WHILE HE WAS IN A DERANGED CONDITION — HOW SIR JAMES MURRAY, EDITOR OF THE DICTIONARY, WHO SET OUT, AS HE THOUGHT, TO VISIT THE HOME OF A FELLOW SAVANT, FOUND HIMSELF AT THE ASYLUM AND HEARD THE EXTRAORDINARY TALE, WHICH BEGINS DURING THE AMERICAN CIVIL WAR, WHEN THE

PRINCIPAL WAS A SURGEON IN THE NORTHERN ARMY —
CONTRIBUTOR WEALTHY AND NOW LIVING IN AMERICA,
SAYS HIS FRIEND.

The breathless headline told of an even more exhausting story
– but one made more than faintly ludicrous by its author's inability
or unwillingness to name Minor. In every reference he is called
simply Dr Blank, as in 'And you, sir, must be Dr Blank. I am most
honoured to meet you . . .'

The story went down well with its American audience, who
had been given hints and snippets of the story in the years before
– the arrest of one of their soldiers for murder in London not
having passed unnoticed at the time, his imprisonment receiving
occasional dustings-off as new correspondents and new diplomats
found their way to London. But the revelation of his work for the
Dictionary was new, and in this regard Hayden Church had a
good, old-fashioned scoop. The wires picked the story up; it
appeared in papers around the world, and as far away as Tientsin
in China.

But in London it did not go down so well. Henry Bradley, who
by this time had taken over from Murray as editor of the Dictionary,
took exception to the *Strand* article. He wrote an angry letter to
the *Daily Telegraph* complaining of the 'several misstatements of
fact', and saying that 'the story of Dr Murray's first interview with
Dr Minor is, so far as its most romantic features are concerned, a
fiction'.

Hayden Church rushed off a spirited reply to Bradley, which
the *Telegraph*, naturally liking a fight, happily published. It contains
vague rebuttals, citing only 'a host of correspondents, some of
them of great eminence' – but none of whom is named – who
had confirmed the major aspects of the story. It pleads, limply,
that 'I have the best of reasons for believing the account of the
meeting between Minor and Murray to be accurate.'

The oddest part of Church's reply, however, is its enigmatic
postscript. 'I have just been in communication with one of the

most distinguished literary men in England, who . . . pointed out
that there did not appear in my article what he personally considered
the most striking feature of all in the American's history.' To that
we shall come later.

Hayden Church's account of the first meeting, whether it was
strictly true or not, turned out to be simply far too good to ignore.
It enthralled all England, people said. It took their mind off the
Great War – 1915, after all, was the year of the second battle of
Ypres, of Gallipoli, of the sinking of the *Lusitania*, and people were
no doubt content to have such a saga as a diversion from the grim
realities of the fighting. 'No romance,' said the *Pall Mall Gazette*,
'is equal to this wonderful story, of scholarship in a padded cell.'

Virtually all subsequent references to the saga of Oxford Diction-
ary-making retell Church's story, to a greater or lesser degree. In
her justly celebrated biography of her grandfather, K. M. Elisabeth
Murray retells Church's version of events almost without question,
as does Jonathon Green in a more general book on the history of
lexicography that was published in 1996. Only Elizabeth Knowles,
an Oxford University Press editor who became intrigued by the
story in the early 1990s, takes a cooler and more detached view:
but she is clearly perplexed that no definitive account of the first
meeting can be found. The patina offered by decades of good use
has made the legend pleasingly credible.

The truth, however, turns out to be only marginally less romantic. It surfaces in a letter that Murray wrote in 1902 to a distinguished
friend, Dr Francis Brown, in Boston, and that turned up in a
wooden box in the attic of one of Minor's very few living relations,
a retired businessman now living in Riverside, Connecticut. The
letter appears to be the original, although it was the exhausting
habit of many letter-writers of the time to prepare a fair copy of
all their outgoing mail, and in doing so occasionally edit and elide
some passages. The letter to Dr Brown appears full and complete.

His first contact with Minor, writes Murray, came very soon
after the beginning of his work on the Dictionary – probably 1880

or 1881. 'He proved to be a very good reader, who wrote to me often,' and, as I have already mentioned, Murray thought only that he must be a retired medical man with plenty of time on his hands.

By accident, my attention was called to the fact that his address, *Broadmoor, Crowthorne, Berkshire,* was that of a large lunatic asylum. I assumed that (perhaps) he was the medical officer of that institution.

But our correspondence was of course entirely limited to the Dictionary and its materials, and the only feeling I had towards him was that of gratitude for his immense help, with some surprise at the rare and expensive old books that he evidently had access to.

This continued for years until one day, between 1887 and 1890, the late Mr Justin Winsor, Librarian of Harvard College, was sitting chatting in my Scriptorium and among other things remarked, 'You have given great pleasure to Americans by speaking as you do in your preface of poor Dr Minor. This is a very painful case.'

'Indeed,' I said with astonishment, 'in what way?'

'Mr W. was equally astonished to find that in all these years I had corresponded with Dr Minor I had never learned nor suspected anything about him; and he then thrilled me with his story.

The great librarian — for Justin Winsor remains one of the grandest figures in all of nineteenth-century American librarianship, and a formidable historian to boot — then told the story, which Murray retells to his friend in Boston. Some of the facts are wrong, as facts tend to be when related over a period of years — Murray says that Minor went to Harvard (while in fact he went to Yale), and repeats the probably apocryphal story that he was driven mad by having to witness the execution of two men after a court martial. He goes on to say that the shooting happened in the Strand — then as now one of London's more fashionable streets — rather than in the grim purlieus of the Lambeth waterside. But essentially the story is relayed correctly, after which Murray resumes his own narrative.

I was of course deeply affected by the story, but as Dr Minor had never in the least alluded to himself or his position, all I could do was to write to him more respectfully and kindly than before, so as to show no notice of this disclosure, which I feared might make some change in our relations.

A few years ago an American citizen who called on me told me he had been to see Dr Minor and said he found him rather low and out of spirits, and urged me to go to see him. I said I shrank from that, because I had no reason to suppose that Dr Minor thought I knew anything about him personally.

He said: 'Yes, he does. He has no doubt that you know all about him, and it really would be a kindness if you would go and see him.'

I then wrote to Dr Minor telling him that, and that Mr (I forget the name) who had recently visited him had told me that a visit from me would be welcome. I also wrote to Dr Nicholson, the then Governor, who warmly invited me – and when I went, drove me from and to the Railway Station and invited me to lunch, at which he also had Dr Minor, who I found was a great favorite with his children.

I sat with Dr Minor in his room or cell many hours altogether before and after lunch, and found him, as far as I could see, as sane as myself, a much cultivated and scholarly man, with many artistic tastes, and of fine Christian character, quite resigned to his sad lot, and grieved only on account of the restriction it imposed on his usefulness.

I learned (from the Governor, I think) that he has always given a large part of his income to support the widow of the man whose death he so sadly caused, and that she regularly visits him.

Dr Nicholson had a great opinion of him, gave him many privileges and regularly took distinguished visitors up to his room or cell, to see him and his books. But his successor the present Governor has not shown such special sympathy.

The meeting took place in January 1891 – six years earlier than is favoured by the romantics who repeat the Dictionary Dinner story. Murray had written to Nicholson asking for permission, and in the letter we can almost feel his child-like knee-squeezing anticipation of the event.

It will give me great satisfaction to make the acquaintance of Dr Minor, to whom the Dictionary owes so much, as well as yourself who have been so kind to him. I shall probably come by the train you name (the 12 from Reading) but have not had time to look up the time-table, or rather to ask my wife to do so; for in such matters I deliver myself automatically into her hands, and she tells me 'Your train starts so and so, and you will go by such a train, and I will come into the Scriptorium and fetch you to get ready five minutes before.' I thankfully comply, and do my work until the 'five minutes before' arrives.

It is now abundantly clear that the two men knew each other personally, and saw each other regularly, for almost twenty years from that date. The first encounter over lunch was to begin a long and firm friendship, based both on a wary mutual respect and, more particularly, on their passionate and keenly shared love for words.

For both men, the first sight of the other must have been peculiar indeed, for they were uncannily similar in appearance. Both were tall, thin and bald. Both had deeply hooded blue eyes, neither using spectacles (though Minor was profoundly myopic). Minor's nose looks a little hooked, Murray's finer, straighter. Minor has an air of avuncular kindliness; Murray much the same, but with a trace of the severity that might well mark a lowland Scot from a Connecticut Yankee.

But their beards and moustaches were the most obvious similarity – in both cases white and long and nicely swallow-tailed beards, with thick moustaches and sideburns and ample bugger grips. Both looked like Father Time; boys in Oxford would see Murray tricycling by and call out 'Father Christmas!' at him.

True, Minor's had a more ragged and unkempt look about it, doubtless because the arrangements for cutting and washing inside Broadmoor were rather less sophisticated than in the outside world. Murray's beard, on the other hand, was fine and well combed and shampooed, and looked as though no particle of food had ever been allowed to rest there. Minor's was the more homely, while Murray's was more of a fashion-statement. But both were magnificently fecund arrangements. When the beards were added to the pair's other individual aspects, each must have imagined, for a second, that he was stepping towards himself in a looking-glass, rather than meeting a stranger.

The two men met dozens of times in the next several years. By all accounts they liked each other – a liking that was subject only to Minor's moods, to which Murray became over the years fully sensible. He often had the foresight to telegraph Nicholson, to ask how the patient was: if low and angry, he would remain at Oxford; if low and likely to be comforted, he would board the train.

When the weather was poor the men would sit together in Minor's small and practically furnished cell, not too dissimilar from a typical Oxford student's room, and just like the room that Murray was to be given at Balliol, once he was made an honorary Fellow. All of its bookshelves were open except for one glass-fronted case that held the rarest of the sixteenth- and seventeenth-century works from which much of the Dictionary work was being done. The fireplace crackled merrily. Tea and Dundee cake were brought in by a fellow inmate whom Minor had hired to work for him – one of the many privileges that Nicholson accorded to his distinguished inmate.

There was a whole raft of other perks besides. He was able to order books at will from various antiquarian dealers in London, New York and Boston. He was able to write uncensored letters to whomever he chose. He was able to have visitors more or less at will – and boasted to Murray with some pride that Eliza Merrett would come to his rooms quite frequently. She was not an unattractive woman, he said, though it was thought that she drank rather too much for comfort.

He subscribed to magazines, which he and Murray would read to each other: the *Spectator* was one of his favourites, and *Outlook*, which was posted to him by his relations in Connecticut. He took the *Athenaeum*, as well as the splendidly arcane Oxford publication *Notes & Queries*, which even today makes puzzling inquiries of the literary community about unsolved mysteries of the bookish world. The Dictionary used to publish its word desiderata there; until the assistants began to write to him with specific queries, this had been his principal means of finding out on which particular words the Dictionary staff were working.

Although the men talked principally about words – most often about a specific word, but sometimes about more general lexical problems of dialect and the nuances of pronunciation – they did, it is certain, discuss in a general sense the nature of the doctor's illness. Murray could not help noticing, for instance, that Minor's cell floor had been covered with a sheet of zinc – 'to prevent men coming in through the timbers at night' – and that he kept a bowl of water beside the door of whichever room he was in – 'because the evil spirits will not dare to cross water to get to me'.

Murray was aware too of the doctor's fears that he would be transported from his room at night and made to perform 'deeds of the wildest excess' in 'dens of infamy' before being returned to his cell by dawn. Once aeroplanes were invented – and Minor, being American, kept keenly up to date with all that happened in the years after the Wright Brothers first flew at Kitty Hawk – he incorporated them into his delusions. Thenceforth, men would break into his rooms, place him in a flying machine and take him to brothels in Constantinople, where he would be forced to perform acts of terrible lewdness with cheap women and small girls. Murray winced as he heard these tales but held his tongue. It was not his place to regard the old man with anything other than sad affection: and besides, his work for the Dictionary continued apace.

On fine-weather days the two men would walk together on the Terrace – a wide gravel path inside the asylum's south wall, shaded by tall old firs and araucaria, the monkey-puzzle tree. The lawns were green, the shrubberies filled with daffodils and tulips; and once in a while other patients would emerge from the blocks to play football, or walk, or sit staring into space from one of the wooden benches. Attendants would lurk in the shadows, making sure there were no outbreaks of trouble.

Murray and Minor, hands behind their backs, would walk in step, slowly back and forth along the 300 yards of the Terrace, in the shadows of either the gaunt red blocks or of the seventeen-foot wall. They always seemed animated, deep in conversation; papers were produced, sometimes books. They did not speak to others, and gave only the impression of inhabiting a world of their own.

Sometimes Dr Nicholson would invite the pair in for afternoon tea; and on one or two occasions Ada Murray would also come to Broadmoor, and remain with Nicholson and his family in the superintendent's comfortably furnished house, while the men pored over the books in the cell or on the gravel walkway. There was always sadness when the time came for the editor to leave: the keys would turn, the gates would clang, and Minor would be left alone again, trapped in a world of his own making, redeemed only when, after a day or so of quiet mourning, he could take down another volume from his shelves, select a needed word and its most elegant context, pick up his pen and dip it in the ink and write once more: *To Dr Murray, Oxford.* The Oxford Post Office knew the address well: it was all that was needed to communicate by letter with the greatest lexicographer in the land, and make sure the information got through to him at the Scriptorium.

Few enough letters between the two men survive. There is a lengthy letter from 1888 in which Minor writes about the quotations containing the word *chaloner* – an obsolete name for a man who manufactured shalloon, which was a woollen lining-material for coats. He is interested, according to a later note, in the word *gondola*, and finds a 1590 quotation from Spenser.

Murray talked about his new friend often, and liked to include him – and indeed, with some discreet reference to his condition – in the speeches he was often obliged to make. In 1897, for instance, his notes survive for a speech he was to give at a Dictionary Evening at the Philological Society:

About 15 or 16,000 add'l slips rec'd during the past year. Half of those supplied by Dr W. C. Minor whose name and pathetic story, I have often before alluded to. Dr M. has in reading 50 or 60 books, mostly scarce, of the 16th–17th C. His practice is to keep just ahead of the actual preparation of the Dictionary.

Two years later Murray felt able to be more copious still:

The supreme position . . . is certainly held by Dr W. C. Minor of Broadmoor, who during the past two years has sent in no less than 12,000 quots. These have nearly all been for the words which Mr Bradley and I were actually occupied, for Dr Minor likes to know each month just what words we are likely to be working on during the month and to devote his whole strength to supplying quotations for those words, and thus to feel that he is in touch with the making of the Dictionary.

So enormous have been Dr Minor's contributions during the past 17 or 18 years, that we could easily illustrate the last 4 centuries from his quotations alone. [my italics]

But the devotion of his whole strength was beginning to prove taxing, both to his body and his mind. His kindly friend Dr Nicholson retired in 1895 – still in pain from being attacked by a patient six years earlier, who hit him on the head with a brick concealed in a sock. He was replaced by Dr Brayn, a man selected by a Home Office that felt a stricter regime needed to be employed at the asylum.

Brayn was indeed a martinet, a gaoler of the old school who would have done well at a prison farm in Tasmania or Norfolk Island. But he did as the government required: there were no escapes during his term of office, and in the first year 200,000 hours of solitary confinement were logged by the more fractious inmates. He was widely feared and loathed by the patients – as well as by Murray, who thought he was treating Minor heartlessly.

And Minor was indeed far from happy. He complains of a hole

in the heel of his sock, doubtless caused by some stranger's shoe into which, at night, he had been obliged to place his foot (November 1896). He is suspicious that his wines and spirits are being tampered with (December 1896).

One curious snippet of information came from America later that same year, when it was noted rather laconically that two of Minor's family had recently killed themselves – the letter going on to warn the staff at Broadmoor that great care should be taken, lest whatever madness gripped their patient turn out to have an hereditary nature. But even if the staff thought Minor a possible suicide risk, no restrictions were placed on him as a result of the American information.

Some years before he had asked for a pocket-knife, with which he might trim the uncut pages of some of the first editions of the books he had ordered: there is no indication that he was asked to hand it back, even with the harsh Dr Brayn in charge. No other patient was allowed to keep a knife: but with his twin cells, his bottles and his books, and his part-time servant, Minor seemed still to belong to a different category from most others in Broadmoor at the time.

In the year following the disclosure about his relations the files speak of Minor taking walks out on the Terrace in all weathers, angrily denouncing those who tried to persuade him to come back in during one especially violent snowstorm, insisting in his imperious way that it was his business alone if he wished to catch cold. He had more freedom of choice and movement than most.

Not that this much improved his temper. A number of old army friends from America happened to come over to London in 1899, and all asked to come to Broadmoor. But the old officer refused to see any of them, saying he did not remember them, and that he did not want to be disturbed. He formally applied to be given some *freedom of the vicinage*, to be let out on parole – the word he used being rather rare, and meaning essentially the same as *the vicinity*.

The elegance of his language convinced no one, however, and his application was firmly denied. 'He is still of unsound mind and I am unable to recommend that his request be granted,' the superintendent wrote to the Home Secretary. (Or typed, it should be said: this is the first document in Minor's file that was produced on a typewriter – an indication that while the patient remained in a miserable stasis, the world around him outside was changing all too rapidly.) The Home Secretary then duly turned down the prayer; on the form is added a bleak initialled notation from the heartless Dr Brayn: 'Patient informed, 12.12.99. R B'.

His diet ticket shows him to be eating fitfully – lots of porridge, sago pudding, custard every Tuesday, but bacon and other meat only occasionally. He appears to have fallen increasingly unhappy, troubled, listless. 'He seems unsettled' is a constant theme of the warders' notes. A visit from Murray in the summer of 1901 cheered him up, but soon afterwards the staff at the Dictionary were beginning to notice a depressing change in their keenest surviving volunteer. 'I notice that he has sent no "Q" quotations,' wrote Murray to a friend. 'But he has been very slack altogether for many months, and I have scarcely heard anything from him. He always is less helpful in summer, because he spends so much more time in the open air, in the garden and grounds. But this year it is worse than usual, and I have been feeling for a good while that I shall have to take a day to go and see him again, and try to refresh his interest . . . In his lonely & sad position he requires a great deal of nursing, encouragement and coaxing, and I have had to go from time to time to see him.'

A month later and things were no better. Murray wrote about him again – by now there are stories of him 'putting his back up' and 'refusing' to do the work that was wanted. He wrote something about the origin of the word *hump*, as on a camel – but aside from that, and coincident with the death of Queen Victoria, he lapsed into a sullen silence.

Another old army friend writing from Northwich in March

1902 asks Superintendent Brayn if he might be allowed to visit Minor, telling him in some distress that Minor himself had written saying that he ought not to, since 'things were much changed, and that I might find it unpleasant'. Please give me your advice, the writer adds: 'I do not wish to expose my wife to anything unpleasant.'

Brayn agreed: 'I do not think it would be advisable for you to visit . . . there are no indications of any immediate danger, but his years are beginning to tell on him . . . his life is precarious.'

It was at about this time that there came the first indication that it might be better if Minor now be allowed to return to the United States, to spend his declining years – as he did seem to be in decline – close to his family.

Minor had been in Broadmoor for thirty years – he was by far the longest-staying patient. He was sustained only by his books. Sadness had utterly enveloped him. He missed the ever sympathetic Dr Nicholson; he was perplexed by the more brutish regime of Dr Brayn. His sole intellectual colleague among the Block 2 patients, the strange artist Richard Dadd, who had been sent to an asylum for stabbing dead his own father, had long since died. His stepmother Judith, whom he had seen briefly in 1885 on her way back from India, had died in New Haven in 1900. Age was fast winnowing out all those who were close to the mad old man.

Even old Fitzedward Hall had died, in 1901 – an event that prompted Minor to fire off a letter of deep and abiding sadness to Murray. Along with his condolences went a request that the editor might perhaps enclose some more slips for the letters 'K' and 'O' – the news of the passing of his fellow countryman seems to have revived Minor's interest in work a little. But only a little. He was now quite alone, in worsening health, harmless to all but himself. He was sixty-seven years old, and showing it. The facts of his circumstances were beginning to weigh heavily on him.

Dr Francis Brown, the distinguished doctor in Boston to whom Murray had written the full account of Minor and their first meeting, thought he might intervene. After hearing from Murray, he had written to the army in Washington and then to the American Embassy in London, and now in March to Dr Brayn, suggesting that – without Minor's knowledge – a petition be sent to the Home Office asking for his release into his family's custody, and his return to America. 'His family would rejoice to have him spend his last days in his own land and nearer to them.'

But the pitiless Brayn did not make the recommendation to the Home Secretary; and neither the embassy nor the army chose to become involved. The old man was to stay put, encouraged only by the occasional correspondence from Oxford, but increasingly dispirited, angry and sad.

A crisis was clearly about to erupt. And erupt it did. The event that in Hayden Church's orotund phrase, was 'the most striking feature of all in the American's history', struck on a cold morning at the beginning of December 1902.

Chapter Ten

The Unkindest Cut

---

masturbate ('mæstɜːbeɪt), v.   [f. I.. masturbāt-,
ppl. stem of masturbārī, of obscure origin: according
to Brugmann for *mastiturbārī f. *mazdo- (cf. Gr.
μέζεα pl.) virile member + turba disturbance. An old
conjecture regarded the word as f. manu-s hand +
stuprāre to defile; hence the etymologizing forms
MANUSTUPRATION, MASTUPRATE, -ATION, used by
some Eng. writers.] intr. To produce an orgasm
by stimulation of the genitals, not by sexual
intercourse . . .

'At 10.55 a.m. Dr Minor came to the bottom gate, which was
locked, and he called out: "You had better send for the Medical
Officer at once! I have injured myself!"'

The words are the first lines on a brief pencilled note lurking
anonymously among the scores of other papers that measure out
the trivial details of the life of Broadmoor's Patient Number 742.
Reports of the more mundane features of William Minor's now
almost solitary life – his diet, his steadily diminishing number of
visitors, his growing frailty, his curmudgeonly lapses, his insane
ruminations – are usually written in ink copperplate, the writing
steady and confident. But this single page, which is dated 3
December 1902, is very different. The fact that it was written in
thick pencil sets it apart – but so does the handwriting, which
makes it look as though it were scrawled urgently by a man who
was breathless, panicky, in a state of shock.

Its author was Block 2 Principal Attendant Mr Coleman. He
had good reason to be appalled by what he was about to see.

I sent Attendant Harfield for the Medical Officer and went to see if I could assist Dr Minor. Then he told me – he had cut his penis off. He said he had tied it with string, which had stopped the bleeding. I saw what he had done.

Dr Baker and Dr Noott then saw him and he was removed to the B-3 Infirmary at 11.30 a.m.

He had taken his walk before breakfast as usual. Also he took his breakfast. I was talking to him at 9.50 in Ward 3, when he appeared to be just as usual.

But he was not in fact 'just as usual' – whatever such a phrase might mean in the context of his well-developed paranoia. Unless his act of self-mutilation was an extraordinary reaction to some equally extraordinary event – which could be true, though there is no proof of it – it looks very much as though Minor had been planning it for several days, if not for months. Cutting off his penis was, by his lights, a necessary and redemptive act: it had probably come about as the consequence of a profound religious awakening, which his doctors believed had begun two years before – or at the end of the century, thirty years after he had been committed.

Minor was the son of missionaries, and he had been brought up, at least notionally, as a staunch Congregationalist Christian. But while at Yale he had largely forsaken his religion, and by the time he was established in the Union Army – whether he had become disillusioned by his experiences on the battlefield, or simply uninterested in organized religion – he apparently abandoned his beliefs totally, and was content to have himself described, without shame, as an atheist.

He was for a while a devoted reader of T. H. Huxley, the great Victorian biologist and philosopher who coined the term *agnostic*. His own feelings were more negative still: since the laws of nature could quite satisfactorily explain all natural phenomena, he would write, he could not find any logical need for the existence of God.

However, over the years in the asylum these feelings of hostility began slowly to ameliorate. By 1898 or so his absolute certainty about the non-existence of God started to waver – perhaps in part because of the strong Christian beliefs of his frequent visitor James Murray, who was the object of Minor's intense and most lasting admiration. Murray may well have discussed the possible solace that Minor might gain from the recognition and acceptance of a superior divinity: unintentionally, he may have triggered what turned out to be Minor's steadily evolving religious intensity.

By the turn of the century Minor had changed: he was telling visitors, and formally informing the Broadmoor superintendent, that he now regarded himself as a deist – as someone who accepts the existence of God but does not subscribe to any particular religion. It was an important step – and yet, in its own way, it was a tragic one.

For in tandem with his new beliefs, Minor began to judge himself by the harsh standards of what he believed to be an all-purpose, all-seeing and eternally vindictive deity. He suddenly stopped thinking of his insanity as a treatable sadness, and instead took to thinking of it – or of some of its aspects – as an intolerable affliction, a state of sin that needed constant purging and punishment. He began to regard himself not as a sorry creature but as someone inexpressibly vile, endowed with terrible habits and leanings. He was a compulsive and obsessive masturbator: God would be certain to punish him dreadfully, should he fail to halt his wholesale dependence on self-abuse.

His prodigious sexual appetites started to become particularly abhorrent to him: he began to be haunted by the memory – or the fantastic supposed memory – of his past sexual conquests. He began to loathe the way his body responded, and the way that God had so inappropriately and unjustly equipped him. As his medical file reported:

He believed there had been a complete saturation of his entire being with the lasciviousness of over 20 years, during which time he had relations with thousands of nude women, night after night. The nightly dissipations had had no perceptible influence on his physical strength, but his organ had increased

in size as the result of such constant use, his constant priapism had allowed it
to develop enormously. He remembers a Frenchwoman remarking 'Bien
fait!' on first seeing it; another woman had called him 'an apostle of pleasure';
sexual adventure and fantasy gave him as much pleasure as anything else in
the world.

But when he became Christianized he saw that he must sever himself from
the lascivious life that he had been leading – and decided that the amputation
of his penis would solve the problem.

The surgical removal of the penis is at the best of times a dangerous
practice, rarely performed even by doctors: an attack by the
renowned bloodsucking Brazilian fishlet known as *candiru*, which
likes to swim up a man's urine stream and lodge in the urethra
with a ring of retrorse spines preventing its removal, is one of
the very rare circumstances in which doctors will perform the
operation, known as a peotomy. It is a brave and foolhardy and
desperate man who will perform an autopeotomy, in which one
removes one's own organ – the more so when the operation is
done in an unsterile environment and with a pen-knife.

Minor's pen-knife had long ceased to be of much use: few were
the occasions when he had to cut the unfinished pages of first
editions, which is why he had asked for the knife in the first place.
Now it just sat in his pocket, as it might in that of an ordinary
man on the outside world. Except that Minor was in no sense
ordinary – and he now had, it turned out, an unusual and pressing
need for the knife.

He was desperately certain that it was his penis that had led him
to commit all the unsavoury deeds that had so dominated his life.
His continuing sexual desires, if not born in his penis, were at least
performed by it. In his delusional world he felt he had no alternative
but to remove it. He was a doctor, of course, and so knew roughly
what he was doing.

So on that Wednesday morning he sharpened his knife on a
whetstone. He tied a thin cord around the base of his member to

act as a ligature and to pressure-cauterize the blood-vessels. He waited for ten minutes or so until the vein and artery walls had become properly compressed – and then, in one swift movement that most would prefer not to imagine, he sliced off his organ about one inch from its base.

He threw the offending object into the fire. He relaxed the string and found that, as he had expected,˙ there was almost no blood. He lay down for a while to ensure there was no haemorrhage – and then walked almost casually to the lower gate on the ground floor of Block 2, and called for the attendant. His training taught him he would probably now go into shock, and he supposed he needed to be put into the asylum infirmary – as indeed the astonished Broadmoor doctors ordered.

He remained there for the best part of a month. Yet within days he was displaying his old cantankerous self, complaining at the noise the workmen were making, even though the day he chose to complain was a Sunday, and the workmen were all at home.

The penis steadily healed, leaving a small stump through which Minor could urinate, but which – to his presumed satisfaction – proved to be useless sexually. The problem had been solved: the deity would be satisfied that no further sexual rompings could take place. The doctor remarked in his ward notes that he was amazed that anyone had the nerve to perform such an extraordinary mutilation on himself.

There remains one further possible reason for his having carried out so bizarre an act – a reason that, since it stretches credulity almost to breaking-point, is mentioned here only for the sake of completeness. He may have amputated his penis out of guilt and self-loathing for having enjoyed either some kind of relationship with, or lascivious thoughts about, the widow of the man he had murdered.

Eliza Merrett, it will be remembered, had visited Minor at the asylum at regular intervals in the early 1880s. She used to bring books and occasional gifts; he and his stepmother had given her money as recompense for her loss; she had said, quite publicly, that she had forgiven him for the murder; she had accepted, sympathetically, that he had committed the crime while not knowing right from wrong. Might it not have been possible that in a moment of mutual consolation – they were almost the same age, and in many senses were in similarly reduced circumstances – something passed between them? And might it not be that, one eventual day, the memory of the event would plunge the sensitive and thoughtful Minor into a deep and guilt-ridden depression?

No suggestion exists that the meetings between Minor and Eliza were anything other than proper, formal and chaste – and perhaps they always were so, and any residual guilt that Minor may have felt stemmed from the kind of fantasies to which his medical records show him to have been prey. But it has to be admitted that it remains a possibility – not a probability, for sure – that it was guilt for a specific act, rather than some slow-burning religious fervour, that prompted this horrible tragedy.

It was exactly a year afterwards that the question of removing Minor to America was raised once again. This time his brother Alfred, who was still running the china emporium back in New Haven, suggested it in a private letter to the superintendent, which Minor never saw. This time, and for the first time, the usually rebarbative Dr Brayn offered some grounds for hope: 'If arrangements could be made for his proper care and treatment, and if the American government would agree to his removal, I think it is quite possible that the proposal might be favourably considered.'

A year later still and Murray visited, on his way back home from seeing his daughter at college in London. He told Brayn that Minor was 'my friend', and said later he was distressed at how frail he seemed, at how the light and energy that had marked him in his Dictionary-busy days of the previous decade seemed now to have deserted him. Murray was further convinced that the old gentleman must be allowed home to die. In England he had no one and no work, no reason for existence. His life was merely a slow-moving tragedy, an act of steady dying conducted before everyone's eyes.

Minor repaid the pleasure of the visit in an unusually intimate way: he gave him a small amount of money. Murray was going off to the Cape Colony, part of what is now South Africa, to attend a conference, and somehow Minor discovered that it was a journey that would stretch Murray's finances to the limit (though the Oxford University Press Delegates gave him a hundred pounds). So Minor decided to pitch in as well, and ordered a postal order for a few pounds, and sent it along with a curiously affectionate note, as one elder might write to another:

Pray pardon the liberty I take, to enclose you a postal payable to your order – that I thought might add in a small way against unexpected demands upon your means.

Even a <u>millionaire</u> may feel satisfaction to find he has a sovereign more than he thought, though himself a republican, and we less gifted people have a right to a like satisfaction when the chance permits.

Building a house and going on a journey are much the same, in costing more than one expects; and in any case I am sure you can make this useful.

Now I will say goodbye to you both, with best wishes for your welfare, and in its uncontracted form also.

God be with you,
W. C. Minor

And over the succeeding weeks and months, so the insane man became steadily the infirm man. He fell in his bath; he hurt his leg; he tripped and twisted leathery sinews and weary muscles; he suffered from the cold and he caught a chill. All the casual inconveniences of old age were being piled on to his madness, each a Pelion upon Ossa, until Minor was no more than a thin and elderly wretch, feared by no one, pitied by all.

Then there came a pathetic example of a smaller madness. Though no longer much of a lexicographer, nor a flautist, Minor remained something of a painter, and filled many hours working at the easel set up in his room. One day, on a whim, he decided he would send one of his better works to the Princess of Wales, the young woman who was wife – Mary of Teck – of the man who would soon become King George V.

But Dr Brayn said no. Bleakly and predictably enforcing the rule that no inmate at Broadmoor may communicate with any member of the Royal Family – a rule made because so many deranged inmates supposed themselves *to be* members of the Royal Family – he told Minor that he could not send it. The doctor, angry and querulous, then formally appealed, forcing Brayn to send the painting and a petition to the Home Office, whose minister had the ultimate say. The office not unnaturally backed Brayn, and Brayn wrote again to Minor, denying him his petition.

But this caused Minor to get his dander up, and he wrote furiously and barely legibly to the American Ambassador, asking that he use his good diplomatic offices to transmit the package to Buckingham Palace. The package was never sent: Brayn insisted he would not allow it. So Minor sent a further letter to the US Army Chief of Staff in Washington, complaining that he, an officer in the US Army himself, was being forcibly prevented from communicating with his embassy.

The whole saga then became the focus of a long summer month's work by a host of attachés and vice-consuls and heads of protocol and assistants to senior staff officers, all bickering and wondering whether this harmless old man's doubtless charming water-colour could ever find its way into the hands of the young – and soon to be elevated to the Queenhood – Princess of Wales.

But it never did. Permission was denied up and down the line – and then ended in a melancholy way. For when Minor sadly retreated to his cell block and asked plaintively for his painting back, he was informed with cold hauteur that it had in fact been lost. The letter asking for the painting is in a spidery, shaky hand – the hand of an elderly, half-sane, half-senile man – and it was to no avail. The painting has never been recovered.

And there were further dispiriting developments. In early March 1910 Dr Brayn – whom history will probably not judge kindly in the specific case of William Minor – ordered that all of the old man's privileges be taken away. Minor was given just a day's notice to quit the suite of two rooms that he had occupied for nearly thirty-eight years, to leave behind his volumes of books, to give up his access to his writing-desk, his sketch-pads and his flutes, and move into the asylum infirmary. It was a cruel outrage committed by a vengeful man, and angry letters poured in from the few remaining friends who heard the news.

Even Ada Murray – now Lady Murray, since James had been knighted in 1908, recommended by a grateful Prime Minister Herbert Asquith – complained bitterly on her husband's behalf about the cruel and cavalier treatment that was apparently being meted out to the 75-year-old Minor. Brayn replied limply that 'I should not have curtailed any of his privileges had I not been convinced that to leave things as they were was running the risk of a serious accident.'

But neither Sir James nor Lady Murray was mollified: it was imperative, they said, that their scholar-genius friend now be allowed to go home to America, out of the clutches of this monstrous Dr Brayn, and away from a hospital that no longer seemed the benign home of harmless scholarship, and more like the Bedlam that it had once been constructed to replace.

His brother Alfred sailed to London in late March with a view to resolving the situation once and for all. He had spoken to the US Army in Washington; the generals there said it was possible, if the British Home Office agreed, to have Minor transferred to a place in which he had been incarcerated very many years before – the Government Hospital for the Insane in the American capital. Provided only that Alfred would keep his brother in safe custody for the transfer across the Atlantic, then the Home Secretary might be persuaded to give his permission.

Fate was to intervene in a merciful way. By great good fortune the Home Secretary of the day was Winston Churchill – a man who, though less well known then than he would soon become, had a naturally sympathetic inclination towards Americans, since his mother was one. He ordered his civil servants to send up a summary of the case to his office – a summary that still exists, and offers a concise and intriguing indication of how governments manage their business.

The various arguments for and against the parole of Minor are offered; the decision is deemed ultimately to rest only on whether, if Minor is still judged to be a danger to others, his brother Alfred can really be 'trusted to keep him away from firearms' during any transfer. The bureaucrats working on the case slowly but inexorably come to parallel understandings: that on the one hand Minor is not dangerous, and that on the other his brother could be well trusted, if needs be. So the recommendation made to Churchill, on the basis of this turgid process of exposition and analysis, was that the man should indeed be released on parole and allowed to go off to his native America.

And so, on Wednesday, 6 April 1910, Winston S. Churchill duly signed, in blue ink, a Warrant of Conditional Discharge, subject only to the condition that Minor 'shall on his discharge leave the United Kingdom and not return thereto'.

The next day Sir James Murray wrote, asking if he might be allowed to say goodbye to his old friend; and if he might bring Lady Murray as well. 'There is not the least objection,' said Dr Brayn smoothly, 'and he is in much better health, and will be pleased to see you.' One can almost hear the lifting of the old man's spirits, with the thought that after thirty-eight long years he was finally going home.

Since the occasion was a momentous one – for Minor but also for England, in more ways than could be immediately understood – Murray had invited an artist from Messrs Russell & Co., Photographers to His Majesty the King, to take a formal farewell portrait of Minor in the Broadmoor asylum garden. Dr Brayn, for once, said he had no objection; the picture that resulted remains a most sympathetic portrait of a kindly, happy and scholarly figure, seemingly seated after tea under a peaceful English hedgerow, unconstrained, untroubled, careless of everything.

At dawn on Saturday, 16 April 1910, Principal Attendant Spanholtz – a lot of Broadmoor attendants, like him, were former Boer War prisoners – was ordered to proceed on escort duty, in plain clothes, to escort Minor to London. Sir James and Lady Murray were there in the weak spring sun to say farewell: there were formal handshakes and, it was said, the glistening of tears.

But these were more dignified times than now; and the two men who had meant so very much to each other for so long, the creation of whose combined scholarship was now almost half complete (the six published volumes of the *New English Dictionary* were packed securely in Minor's valise), said goodbye to one another in an air of stiff formality. Dr Brayn offered his own curt valedictory; the landau rattled its way down the lanes, soon becoming lost in an early spring mist. Two hours later it was at Bracknell Station, on the south-east main line for London.

An hour later Spanholtz and Minor were at the mighty vaulting cathedral of Waterloo Station – a much larger station now than it had been when, no more than a few hundred yards away, the murder that began this story had been committed on that Saturday night in 1872. The pair did not linger, for obvious reasons, but took a hansom cab to St Pancras and there caught the boat-train to Tilbury Docks. They walked to the quayside, where the Atlantic Transport Line's twin-screw passenger liner SS *Minnetonka* lay, coaling and victualling, bound that afternoon for New York.

It was only at the dockside that the Broadmoor attendant finally relinquished custody of his charge, and handed him over to Alfred Minor, who was waiting beside the ship's gangway. A receipt was duly offered and signed, just before noon, as though the patient were a large box, or a haunch of meat. 'This is to certify that William Chester Minor has this day been received from the Broadmoor

Criminal Lunatic Asylum into my care,' it read, and it was signed 'Alfred W. Minor, Conservator'.

The Broadmoor attendant waved his own cheery goodbye, and raced off to catch his return train. At two o'clock the vessel blasted a farewell on her steam-horn and, with tugs yelping, edged out into the estuary of the River Thames. By mid-afternoon she was off the North Foreland and had turned hard to starboard; by nightfall she was in the Channel; by dawn on the next fresh morning she was south of the Scilly Isles; and by lunchtime all England and the nightmare that she enfolded had finally receded, lost, over the damp taffrail. The sea was grey and huge and empty; and ahead lay America, and home.

Two weeks later Dr Brayn received a note from New Haven.

I am glad to say that my brother safely made the trip, and is now pleasantly fixed in the St Elizabeth's Asylum in Washington, DC. He enjoyed the voyage very much and had no trouble from sea-sickness. I thought he walked about too much for the latter part of the voyage. He did not trouble me at night – though I felt much relief on arriving at the dock in New York . . . I hope I have the pleasure of meeting you at some future date. My regards to yourself and your family, and best wishes to all the Broadmoor staff and attendants.

Chapter Eleven

Then Only the Monuments

---

diagnosis (daɪəg'nəʊsɪs). Pl. **-oses**. [a. L. *diag-
nōsis*, Gr. διάγνωσις, n. of action f. διαγιγνώσκειν
to distinguish, discern, f. δια- through, thoroughly,
asunder + γιγνώσκειν to learn to know, perceive. In
F. *diagnose* in Molière: cf. prec.]
     1. a. *Med.* Determination of the nature of a diseased
condition; identification of a disease by careful investigation of its symptoms and history; also, the opinion
(formally stated) resulting from such investigation.

Old Frederick Furnivall was the first of the great Dictionary men
to go. He died within just a few weeks of the *Minnetonka* sailing
away from London, and bearing Minor back to America.

Furnivall had known he was dying since the beginning of that
fateful year, 1910. He remained amusing and energetic to the end,
sculling his little boat at Hammersmith, sending his daily packages
of words and newspaper clippings to the editor of a project with
which he had been intimately associated for all of half a century.

He started his letter to Murray with a typically eccentric disdain
for the illness that he knew would shortly fell him. His first
expressed interest was in a word – *tallow catch* – that Murray had
found in Shakespeare, had recently defined and had sent down to
Hammersmith for approval: Furnivall offered his congratulations
for a definition that read in part 'a very fat man . . . a tub of tallow',
a word that has similarities today with a reference to a man as *a
tub of lard*. It was only after this that he spoke elliptically of the
grim prognosis his doctor had offered – he turned out to have
intestinal cancer – and remarked, 'Yes, our Dict. Men go gradually,

& I am to disappear in six months . . . It's a great disappointment, as I wanted to see the Dict. finished before I die. But it is not to be. However the completion of the work is certain. So that's all right.'

He died as predicted, in July, but he did not abandon his labours until after inspecting, as Murray had suggested that he might, one majestically long entry that was due for inclusion in *Volume XI*. 'Would it give you any satisfaction,' Murray had asked him, 'to see the gigantic TAKE in final? Before it is too late?'

Murray himself knew that, with Furnivall's passing, his own end could not be too far off. And with his offer of *take* to Furnivall, it was evident he had only just begun the monumental work on the entirety of the letter 'T'. That single letter was to take him five long years to complete, from 1908 until 1913. When he finished he was so relieved as to voice an incautiously optimistic forecast: 'I have got to the stage where I can estimate the end. In all human probability the Dictionary will be finished on my eightieth birthday, four years from now.'

But no. Neither was the Dictionary to be completed in four years, nor was Sir James ever to become an octogenarian. The Grand Conjunction for which he hoped – his own Golden Wedding, his Dictionary's completion – never happened. Oxford's Regius Professor of Medicine once joked that the university seemed to be paying him a salary 'just to keep that old man alive' so he could complete his work. They did not, it seems, pay enough.

His prostate gave up on him in the spring of 1915, and the burning X-rays with which such problems were then treated hurt him severely. He kept up his pace of work, completing *trink* to *turndown* in mid-summer, and including many difficult words that, as a fellow editor said, 'were handled with characteristic sagacity and resource'. He was photographed for the last time in the Scriptorium on 10 July – his staff and daughters around and behind him, and in the background shelves of bound books replacing the pigeon-holes with their thousands of slips of paper, which had been the familiar backdrop in the Dictionary's earlier days. Sir James has his academic cap still atop his head, but he looks thin and weary; his expression is of calm resignation, the expressions of those beside him knowing and tragic.

He died on 26 July 1915, of pleurisy, and was buried as he wished to be, beside a great Oxford friend who had been Professor of Chinese.

Minor, now into his fifth year at the Government Hospital for the Insane in Washington, DC, would have heard in due course of the death of the man who had brought him so much solace and intellectual comfort. But on the actual day of Murray's passing he merely had yet another of the bad days that he was increasingly now enduring. Some might say that it was a day on which Minor in Washington was unknowingly in sympathy with the sad events that were unfolding in Oxford, more than 3,000 miles across the Atlantic Ocean.

'Struck one of his fellow patients,' read the notes of Minor's Cherry Ward for that same Monday evening, 26 July. 'He had happened to stop and look into his room. Shows temper and will try to strike hard, but has little strength to hurt anyone.' (He had started hitting people the month before. He went walking one June afternoon, along with his attendant, and the pair met a policeman. When the officer began to ask questions, Minor started pounding the attendant on the chest – though he later said he was sorry, and explained that he was becoming 'a little excitable'.)

He had probably been capable of inflicting little hurt from the moment he was first entered in the hospital log. He may have been mad, but he was painfully slender, his spine was bowed, he shuffled as he walked, he had lost his teeth and had alopecia. He had photographs taken, full on and in profile, as if he were a common criminal: his beard is long and white, his bald head high and domed, his eyes wild. His madness was defined as simple paranoia, the doctors said; he admitted that he still thought constantly about little girls, and that he had dreams about the appalling acts that they forced him to perform during his forced nightly excursions.

But he was not regarded as dangerous: his doctors agreed that he should be granted the privilege of walking into the surrounding countryside, if accompanied by an attendant. The stump of his penis attested dramatically to the fact that he should not be allowed access to either a knife or to scissors. But otherwise, he was deemed harmless – he was just an 81-year-old man, thin, toothless, wrinkled, slightly deaf and only 'very active, considering his age'.

His delusions steadily worsened during the St Elizabeth's years. He complained that his eyes were regularly pecked out by birds, that people forced food into his mouth through a metal funnel and then hammered on his fingernails, that scores of pygmies hid beneath the floorboards of his room and acted as agents for the Underworld. He was occasionally irritable, but more usually quiet and courteous, and he read and wrote a great deal in his room. He had a somewhat arrogant air, said one doctor; he did not much care for the company of his fellow patients, and he would absolutely not let any one of them go into his private room.

It was at St Elizabeth's that his hitherto puzzling illness was given what might be regarded as its first modern, currently recognizable description. On 8 November 1918 his attending psychiatrist, a Dr Davidian, formally declared that William Minor, Federal Patient Number 18487, was suffering from what was to be called 'dementia praecox, of the paranoid form'. No longer was the vague word monomania to be used, nor would simple paranoia do. Minor and his case-history had been finally cast off from the dubious moorings of the Victorians' puzzled but determinedly 'moral treatment' of the mad – the phrase had been coined by the Frenchman Philippe Pinel of La Salpêtrière in Paris – and were at last to be welcomed into the world of modern psychiatry.

The new phrase, dementia praecox, was quite precise. By the time

Davidian employed it as a diagnosis it had been current for twenty years. It literally meant 'early-flowering failure of the mental powers', and was used to distinguish a condition in which a person begins to lose touch with reality, as Minor had done, early on in his life – in his teens, his twenties or his thirties. In this sense the illness was markedly different from *senile dementia*, a term once used to describe the decrepitude that specifically accompanies old age, and of which Alzheimer's Disease is one kind.

The nomenclature was published in Heidelberg in 1899 by the German psychiatrist Emil Kraepelin, who at the time was the supreme classifier of known mental ills. His naming of the condition was designed less to distinguish it from being an old person's ailment, as to mark it as very different from *manic-depressive psychosis*, an illness that had enough similarities to confuse the earliest of the alienists.

Kraepelin's view, revolutionary at the time, was that while manic-depressive psychoses had identifiable physical causes (such as a low level of the alkali metal lithium in the blood and brain), and were thus treatable (as with the use of lithium, for example, to top up a depressive's lack of it), *dementia praecox* was a so-called endogenous ailment, quite lacking in any identifiable external cause. In that respect it was to be regarded as similar to such enigmatic systemic physical disorders as essential hypertension, in which a patient develops high blood pressure – and its many untidy and inconvenient side effects – for no obvious reason.

Kraepelin went on to define three distinct sub-types of *dementia praecox*. There was *catatonic*, in which the motor functions of the body are either excessive or non-existent; *hebephrenic*, where grotesquely inappropriate behaviour begins during puberty, hence the word's origin from the Greek ἥβη, youth; and *paranoiac*, in which the victim suffers from delusions, often of persecution. It was from this kind of dementia, according to Kraepelin's classification of the time, that Minor was suffering.

The traditional treatment offered to him and his kind was still simple, basic and, by today's standards, dismayingly unenlightened. Those suffering from paranoid dementia were deemed pathologically incurable, were removed from society by order of court and were placed – kindly, tenderly, for the most part, thanks to Pinel's powerful influence – in cells behind high walls, so as to cause no inconvenience to those living in the normal, outside world. Some were incarcerated for only a very few years; some for ten or twenty. In the case of Minor his involuntary exile from society was to last for most of his life. He existed for most of his first thirty-eight years on the outside, until he killed George Merrett. Then for forty-seven of the forty-eight years that were left to him he was locked away in state asylums, essentially untreated because he was, in the view of the doctors of the day, essentially untreatable.

Since the time of Minor and Davidian the illness has become much more liberally regarded. Its name, for a start, has changed: what was initially the far less daunting word *schizophrenia* – it came from the Greek for *split mind* – made its first appearance in 1912. (It may change again: to rid the ailment of its patina of unpleasant associations, there are now moves to have it called Kraepelin's Syndrome.)

Early treatments for the disease, which were just being introduced at the time of Minor's final decline, involved the use of massive sedatives like chloral hydrate, sodium amytal and paraldehyde. Today entire shelves of costly anti-psychotic drugs are available to at least treat and manage schizophrenia's more discomforting symptoms. But so far, and despite the spending of fortunes, there have been precious few advances in staying the mysterious triggers that seemingly set off the illness and its demonic mischiefs.

And there continues to be much debate about what these triggers might be. Can it ever be said that a major psychological illness like schizophrenia, with its severe disruption of the brain's chemistry, appearance and function, truly has a *cause*? In the case of Minor –

could the terrible scenes at the Battle of the Wilderness actually have triggered his florid behaviour?

Might his branding of an Irishman have precipitated, led directly, or contributed even indirectly, to the crime that he committed eight years later, and that led to the exile he was to suffer for the remainder of his life? Was there ever an identifiable happening, was he ever exposed to the mental equivalent of an invading germ? Or is schizophrenia truly causeless, a part of the very being of some unfortunate individuals? Moreover, what is the illness – is it simply the development of a personality that is several steps beyond mere eccentricity, and that steps into areas which society does not find itself able to tolerate or approve of?

No one is quite certain. In 1984 a paper was presented describing a man who firmly believed himself to have two heads. He found one of them irritating beyond endurance, and shot at it with a revolver, injuring himself terribly in the process. He was diagnosed as schizophrenic, and the psychiatric community agreed, since it was manifestly certain that the man only had one head, and suffered and was dominated by an absurd delusion. But then again, the notorious 'Mad Lucas' of Victorian Hertfordshire – who lived with his wife's dead body for three months, then by himself, in wild biblical solitude and squalor for the next quarter century, and was visited by coachloads of trippers up from London for the day – was diagnosed as schizophrenic too. Should he have been? Was he not merely a borderline eccentric, behaving in a fashion beyond the accepted norms? Was he as mad as the deluded owner of the phantom head? Was he as dangerous, and as deserving of confinement? And how does a case like Minor's sit within the spectrum of this madness? Was he less mad than the first man, and more so than the second? How does one quantify? How does one treat? How does one judge?

Psychiatrists today remain cautious about all of these questions, and remain puzzled and argumentative about whether the illness can be triggered, whether it does have a definable cause. Most academic psychiatrists hedge their bets, avoiding dogma, preferring simply to say they believe in 'the cumulative effect of a number of factors'.

A patient may have a simple genetic predisposition to the illness. Or he may have characteristics of his basic temperament that similarly increase the likelihood that he will 'react badly' or floridly to an external stress – to the sights of a battlefield, to the shock of a torture. But perhaps certain sights and the ensuing shocks are too great, or too sudden, for anyone to endure them and remain wholly sane.

There is the newly recognized condition known as Post-Traumatic Stress Disorder, which seems to affect inordinately large numbers of people who have been exposed to truly appalling situations. The only difference between their cases today, after the Gulf War where it was first identified *en masse*, or after the trauma of a kidnap or a traffic accident, and those of the past is that most sufferers become relieved of their symptoms after a period of time. William Chester Minor never was. His agony endured for his entire life. However convenient it may be to say that Post-Traumatic Stress ruined his life, and that of his victim, the continuing symptoms suggest otherwise. There was something wildly wrong with his brain, and what happened in Virginia probably prompted its more ruinous manifestations to emerge.

Perhaps it was an unusual genetic make-up that predisposed him to fall ill – two of his relations had killed themselves, after all, though we are not certain of the circumstances. Maybe his gentle temperament – he was a painter, a flautist, a collector of old books – made him unusually vulnerable to what he saw and felt on those blood-soaked fields in the South. Maybe his subsequent imprisonment in Broadmoor then left him unimproved, when a more compassionate and enlightened regime might have mitigated his darker feelings, might have helped him recover. One in a hundred people today suffers from schizophrenia: nearly all of them, if treated with compassion and good chemistry, can make a fist of some kind of dignified life, of a kind that was denied, for much of his time, to Minor.

Except, of course, that Minor had his Dictionary work. And there is a cruel irony in this – that had he been treated with today's compassion and good chemistry, he may never have felt impelled to work on it as he did. By offering him mood-altering sedatives, as they would have done in Edwardian times, or treating him as today with such anti-psychotic drugs as Quetiapine or Risperidone, many of his symptoms of madness might have gone away – but he might well have felt disinclined or unable to perform his work for Murray.

In a way, those Dictionary slips *were* his medication, they became his therapy. The routine of his quiet and cell-bound intellectual stimulus, month upon month, year upon year, appears to have provided him with at least a measure of release from his paranoia. His sad situation only worsened when that stimulus was gone: when the great book ceased to function as his lodestone, when the one fixed point on which his remarkable but tortured brain was able to concentrate became detached, so then he began to spiral downwards, and his life to ebb.

One must feel a sense of strange gratitude that his treatment was never good enough to divert him from his work. The agonies that he must have suffered in those terrible asylum nights have granted us all a benefit, for all time. He was mad, and for that we have reason to be glad. A truly savage irony, on which it is discomfiting to dwell.

In November 1915, four months after Sir James had died, Minor wrote to Lady Murray in Oxford, offering her all the books that had been sent from Broadmoor to the Scriptorium, and that had been in Sir James's possession when he died. He hoped they might eventually go off to the Bodleian Library. 'I am glad . . . to know that you are well, as I must presume from your letter and occupations. You must be taking or giving a great deal of labour for Dict'y materials still.' And his books do indeed rest in the great library to this day: they are registered as having been donated 'By Dr Minor through Lady Murray'.

But by now he was failing steadily. An old colleague from Civil War days wrote from West Chester, Pennsylvania, to ask how his friend was – and the hospital superintendent replied that, considering his years, Captain Minor was in good health, and was in a 'bright and cheerful ward, where he seems contented with his surroundings'.

But the ward notes tell a different story, presenting as they do a litany of all the symptoms of the steady onset of senility and dementia. With increasing frequency the attendants write of Minor stumbling, injuring himself, getting lost, losing his temper, wandering, growing dizzy, tiring easily – and, worst of all, beginning to forget, and to know that he was forgetting. His mind, though tortured, had always been peculiarly acute: now, by 1918 and the end of the Great War, he seemed to understand that his faculties were dimming, that his mind was at last becoming as weakened as his body, and that the sands were running out. For days at a time he would stay in bed, saying he needed 'a good rest'; he would barricade the door with chairs, certain in his persecution. It was more than forty-five years since the murder, fully half a century since the first signs of madness had been noticed, back at the Florida army fort. And yet the symptoms remained the same, persistent, uncured, uncurable.

Still came the occasional querulous note, such as this, written in the summer of 1917:

Dr White – Dear Sir, There was a time when the meat – beef and ham – was very tough and dry. This has in a degree altered for the better since your note even, and I would not complain of that: and rice seemed to be the only vegetable with it.

This is not much to complain of: and yet these trifles are much to us in this life.

Thanking you for what you would wish to do.

I am very truly yours

W. C. Minor

A year later – though his failing memory and eyesight cause him to date the letter 1819 rather than 1918 – he shows another strange spurt of benevolence, similar to his contributing to Murray's adventure to the Cape. In this latest case he sent twenty-five dollars to the Belgian Relief Fund, and a further twenty-five to Yale University, his alma mater, as a donation to its military service fund. The Yale President wrote back from Woodbridge Hall: 'I have known much of Dr Minor's history,' he replied to the superintendent, 'and am therefore doubly touched to receive this gift.'

In 1919 his nephew, Edward Minor, applied to the army to have him released from St Elizabeth's and brought to a hospital for the elderly insane in Hartford, Connecticut, known as the Retreat. The army agreed: 'I think if the Retreat fully understands the case we should let him go,' said a Dr Duval, at an October conference to discuss the matter. 'He is getting so old now he will probably not do much harm.' The hospital board agreed too, and in November, in a snowstorm, the frail old gentleman left Washington, and the strange world of insane asylums – a world that he had inhabited since 1872 – for good.

He liked his new home, a mansion set in acres of woods and gardens on the banks of the Connecticut River. His nephew wrote in the early winter of 1920 of how the change seemed to have done him some good, and yet at the same time of how incapable he was of looking after himself. Furthermore, he was fast going blind, and for some months had been unable to read. With this one overarching source of joy now denied to him, there must have been little left to live for. No one was surprised when, after a walk on a blustery early spring day in that same year, he caught a cold that turned into bronchiopneumonia, and died peacefully in his sleep. It was Friday, 26 March 1920. He had lived for eighty-five years and nine months. He might have been mad, but, like Dr Johnson's *Dictionary* elephant, he had been *extremely long lifed*.

There were no obituaries: just two lines in the Deaths columns of the *New Haven Register*. He was taken down to his old hometown and buried in the Evergreen Cemetery on the afternoon of the following Monday, in the family plot that had been established by his missionary father, Eastman Strong Minor. The gravestone is small and undistinguished, made of reddish sandstone, and bears only his name. An angel stands on a plinth near by, gazing skywards, with the engraved motto, *My faith looks up to Thee*.

Around the Evergreen Cemetery a high chain-link fence keeps out an angry part of New Haven, well away from the stern elegance of Yale. The simple existence of the fence underlines a sad and ironic reality: Dr William Chester Minor, who was among the greatest of contributors to the finest dictionary in all the English language, died forgotten in obscurity, and is buried near a slum.

The *New English Dictionary* itself took another eight years to finish, the announcement of its completion made on New Year's Eve, 1927. *The New York Times* put the fact on the front page next New Year's morning, a Sunday – that with the inclusion of the old Kentish word *zyxt* – the second singular indicative present tense, in local argot, of the verb *to see* – the work was done, the alphabet exhausted, and the full text now wholly in the printers' hands. The making of the great book, declared the newspaper roundly and generously, was 'one of the great romances of English literature'.

The Americans did indeed love the story of its making. H. L. Mencken – no mean lexicographer himself – wrote that he fully expected Oxford to celebrate the culmination of the seventy-year project with 'military exercises, boxing matches between the dons, orations in Latin, Greek, English and the Oxford dialect, yelling matches between the different Colleges and a series of medieval drinking bouts'. Considering that the final editor of the book had held professorships at both Oxford and Chicago, there was more than good reason for Americans to take a keen interest in a creation that was now, at least partly, of their own making.

The lonely drudgery of lexicography, the terrible undertow of words against which men like Murray and Minor had so ably struggled and stood, now had at last its great reward. Twelve mighty volumes; 414,825 words defined; 1,827,306 illustrative quotations used, to which Minor alone had contributed scores of thousands.

The total length of type – all handset, for the books were done by letterpress, still discernible in the delicately impressed feel of the inked-on paper – is 178 miles, the distance between London and the outskirts of Manchester. Discounting every punctuation mark and every space – which any printer knows occupies just as much time to set as does a single letter – there are no fewer than 227,779,589 letters and numbers.

Other dictionaries in other languages took longer to make; but none was greater, grander or had more authority than this. The greatest effort since the invention of printing. The longest sensational serial ever written.

One word – and only one word – was ever actually lost: *bondmaid*, which appears in Johnson's *Dictionary*, was actually mislaid by Murray and found, a stray without a home, long after the fascicle *Battentlie–Bozzom* had been published. It, and tens of thousands of words that had evolved or appeared during the forty-four years spent assembling the fascicles and their parent volumes, appeared in a supplement, which came out in 1933. Four further supplements appeared between 1972 and 1986. In 1989, using the new abilities of the computer, Oxford University Press issued its fully integrated second edition, incorporating all the changes and additions of the supplements in twenty rather more slender volumes. Then came a CD-ROM, and not long afterwards the great work was further adapted for use on-line. A third edition, with a vast budget, is in hand.

There is some occasional carping that the work reflects an elitist, male, British and Victorian tone. Yet even in the admission that, like so many achievements of the era, it did reflect a series of attitudes that are not wholly harmonic with those at the end of the twentieth century, none seems to suggest that any other dictionary has ever come close, or will ever come close, to the achievement that it offers. It was the heroic creation of a host of interested and enthusiastic men and women of wide general knowledge and interest; and it lives on today, as does the language of which it rightly claims to be a portrait.

Chapter Twelve

Postscript

---

memorial (mɪ'mɔərɪəl), *a.* and *sb.* [a. OF. *mem-orial* (mod.F. *mémorial*) = Sp., Pg. *memorial*, It. *memo-riale*, ad. L. *memoriālis* adj. (neut. *memoriāle*, used in late Latin as sb.), f. *memoria* MEMORY.] **A.** *adj.*
　　1. Preserving the memory of a person or thing . . .
　　3. Something by which the memory of a person, thing, or event is preserved, as a monumental erection . . .

This has been the story of an American soldier whose involvement in the making of the world's greatest dictionary was singular, astonishing, memorable and laudable – and yet at the same time wretchedly sad. And in the telling, it is tempting to forget that the circumstances that placed William Chester Minor in the position from where he was able to contribute all his time and energy to the making of the *OED* began with his horrible and unforgivable commission of a murder.

George Merrett, who was his victim, was an ordinary, innocent working-class farmer's son from Wiltshire, who came up to London to make his living, but who was shot dead, leaving a pregnant wife, Eliza, and six young children. The family were already living in the direst poverty, trying to maintain some semblance of their farm-country dignity among the squalor of one of the roughest and most unforgiving parts of the Victorian city. Matters now took a terrible turn for the worse.

All London was shocked and horrified by the killing, and funds were raised and money collected to help the widow and her brood.

Americans in particular, stunned at the outrage committed by one of their own, were asked by their Consul-General to contribute to a diplomatic fund; the vicars in Lambeth banded together to make collections, ecumenically; a series of amateur entertainments – including one 'of an unusually high-class character' with readings of Longfellow and of a selection from *Othello*, and held at the Hercules Club – was staged across town to raise money; and the funeral itself was a splendid affair, as impressive as that of any grandee.

George Merrett had been a member of the Ancient Order of Foresters – one of the many so-called Friendly Societies that were once popular across Britain as a means, in the absence of any government or privately funded schemes, of providing co-operative pensions and other financial help for the working classes. On the night that he died Merrett had been relieving a shift-worker who was a brother Forester: this act of small benevolence made the Order doubly obliged to offer their late member a handsome farewell.

The cortège was half a mile long: the Foresters' Band playing the 'Funeral March' from *Saul* came first, then scores of emblem-wearing members, then the horse-drawn hearse and four black mourning-coaches to carry the bereaved. Eliza Merrett rode in the leading carriage, holding her youngest baby in her arms, and sobbing. Hundreds of brewery workers followed, and then thousands of ordinary members of the public, all wearing black crêpe bands around their arms or hats.

The procession wound for the entire afternoon from Lambeth, past the spot on Belvedere Road where the tragedy had occurred, past the Bedlam Hospital and up to the vast cemetery at Tooting, where George Merrett was finally buried.

His grave may have once been marked, but it lacks a marker now, and where the records say George Merrett lies there is no more than a patch of discoloured grass, a tiny patch of settled earth among a sea of more noble and newer monuments.

In his lucid moments Minor was contrite, appalled by the consequences of his moment of mad delusion. But Eliza never really recovered from the shock of the murder: she took to drink, and when she died it was of liver failure. There is no grave.

Two of her sons' lives unravelled most curiously: George, the second eldest boy, took a gift of money from Minor's stepmother to Monaco, won a considerable sum and remained there, styling himself the King of Monte Carlo, before dying in impoverished obscurity in the South of France. His younger brother Frederick shot himself dead in London, for reasons that have never been fully explained. The fact that two of Minor's brothers also died by their own hand invests the entire story with more sadness than is bearable.

But the principal tragic figure in this strange tale is the man who is the least well remembered, and who was gunned down on the damp and cold cobblestones of Lambeth on that Saturday night in February 1872.

The only public memorials ever raised to the two most tragically linked of this saga's protagonists are miserable, niggardly affairs. Minor has just a simple little gravestone in a New Haven cemetery, hemmed in between litter and slums. George Merrett has for years had nothing at all, except for a patch of greyish grass in a sprawling graveyard in south London. Minor does, however, have the advantage of the great Dictionary, which some might say acts as his most lasting remembrance. But nothing else remains to suggest that the man he killed was ever worthy of any memory at all. George Merrett has become an absolutely unsung man.

Which is why it now seems fitting, more than a century and a quarter on, that this modest account begins with the dedication that it does. And why this book is offered as a small testament to the late George Merrett of Wiltshire and Lambeth, without whose untimely death these events would never have unfolded, and this tale could never have been told.

Author's Note

|| **coda** ('koda, 'kəʊdə).   [Ital.:–L. *cauda* tail.]
   1. *Mus.* A passage of more or less independent
character introduced after the completion of the
essential parts of a movement, so as to form a more
definite and satisfactory conclusion. Also *transf.* and
fig.

I first became intrigued by the central figure of this story, the
Dictionary itself, back in the early 1980s, when I was living in
Oxford. One summer's day a friend who worked at the University
Press invited me into a warehouse to look at a forgotten treasure.
It was a jumbled pile of plates of metal, each one measuring a little
over seven inches by ten, and – as I found when I picked one up
– as heavy as the devil.

They were discarded letterpress printing plates: the original
lead-fronted, steel-and-antimony-backed plates, cast in the nineteenth and early twentieth centuries, from which all of the many
printings of the *OED* – from the individual fascicles produced as the
books were being edited, to the final twelve-volume masterpiece of
1928 – had been made.

The Press, my friend explained, had recently adopted more
modern methods, computer typesetting and photolithography and
the like. The old ways of the letterpress men, with their slugs of
lead and their typesticks, their em-quads and their brasses and
coppers, their tympan paper and their platen brushes and their
uncanny ability to read backwards and upside-down at speed, were
at long last being abandoned. The plates, and all the job-cases of

type for handsetting, were now being tossed away, melted down, carried off.

Would I perhaps like one or two of the plates, he asked me – just to keep as souvenirs, of something that had once been rather marvellous?

I chose three of them, reading the backwards type as best I could in the dim and dusty light. Two of them I later gave away. But I kept one: it was the complete page 452 of the great Dictionary's *Volume V*: it encompassed the words *humoral* to *humour*, it had been edited in 1901 or so, and set in type in 1902.

For years I took the strange, dirty-looking old plate around with me. It was a kind of talisman. I would squirrel it away in cupboards in the various flats and houses in the various cities and villages in which I came to live. I was rather proud of it – boringly so, I dare say – and every so often I would find it hidden behind other, more important things, and I would bring it out, blow off the dust and show it off to friends, a small and fascinating item of lexicographic history.

I am sure at first they thought I was a little mad – though in truth I fancy they seemed after a while to understand my odd affection for the blackened and *so heavy!* little thing. I would watch as they would rub their fingers gently over its raised lead, and nod in mute agreement: the plate seemed to offer them some kind of tactile pleasure, as well as the simpler intellectual amusement.

When I came to live in America in the mid-nineties I met a letterpress printer, a woman who lived in western Massachusetts. I told her about the plate, and she became visibly excited. She had a great enthusiasm for the story of the making of the Dictionary, she said, as well as a tremendous fondness for its design – for the elegant and clever mix of typography and font sizes that the stern old Victorian editors had employed. She asked to see my plate, and when I brought it for her, she asked if she might borrow it for a while.

That while turned into two years, during which time she took on as much other work as a hand-printer gets these days. She embarked on a series of broadsides for John Updike, made chap-books for a couple of other New England poets, published a collection or two of short stories and plays, all of which she had printed on handmade paper. She was very much the craftswoman, all her work meticulous, slow, perfect. And she kept my dictionary plate standing on a windowsill all the while, wondering what best to do with it.

Finally she decided. She knew that I had a great liking for China, and had lived there for many years; and that I was also more fond of Oxford than of any other English city. So she took down the plate, washed it carefully in a range of solvents to purge it of its accumulated dust and grease and ink, she mounted it on her Vandercook proof printer, and carefully pressed, on the finest hand-wove paper, two editions of the page – one inked in Oxford Blue, the other in China Red.

She then mounted the three items side by side – the metal plate in the middle, one red page to the left, the other blue page to the right – and set them inside a slender gold frame, behind non-reflecting glass. She left the completed picture, with wire and bracket for hanging it on the wall, in a small café in her hometown, and then wrote a postcard telling me to pick it up whenever I could, and at the same time to take care to enjoy the café-owner's strawberry and rhubarb pie, and her cappuccino. There was no bill; and I have never seen the printer since.

But the plate and its proof sheets hang on my wall still, above a small lamp that illuminates an open volume of the great Dictionary on the desk below. It is *Volume V*, and I keep it open to the same page that was once printed from the actual piece of metal that hangs suspended just above it. It is what Victorians would have called a Grand Conjunction, and it serves as a small shrine to the pleasures of book-making and printing, and to the joy of words.

Once my mother noticed that the dominant entry on the plate and the sheets and in the book below is the word *humorist*. It reminded her of a nicely droll coincidence, another Conjunction, though one rather less Grand. *Humorist* had been the name of a horse that ran in the Derby on 1 June 1921, the day that my mother was born. Her father, so pleased at the news of the birth of a baby girl, had put ten guineas on the animal, rank outsider though she was. But she won, and a grandfather whom I never met made a thousand guineas, and all because of a word that briefly took his fancy.

Acknowledgements

---

acknowledgment (æk'nɒlɪdʒmənt). Also **acknowledgement** (a spelling more in accordance with Eng. values of letters). [f. ACKNOWLEDGE *v.* + -MENT. An early instance of *-ment* added to an orig. Eng. vb.]

    1. The act of acknowledging, confessing, admitting, or owning; confession, avowal . . .

    5. The owning of a gift or benefit received, or of a message; grateful, courteous, or due recognition . . .

    6. Hence, The sensible sign, whereby anything received is acknowledged; something given or done in return for a favour or message, or a formal communication that we have received it.

    1739 T. SHERIDAN *Persius* Ded. 3. I dedicate to you this Edition and Translation of Persius, as an Acknowledgment for the great Pleasure you gave me. 1802 M. EDGEWORTH *Moral T.* (1816) I. xvi. 133 To offer him some acknowledgment for his obliging conduct. 1881 *Daily Tel.* Dec. 27 The painter had to appear and bow his acknowledgments. *Mod.* Take this as a small acknowledgement of my gratitude.

When I first came upon this story, which was mentioned all too briefly, just as an aside, in a rather sober book about the dictionary-making craft, it struck me immediately as a tale that was worth investigating, and perhaps telling in full. But for several months I was alone in thinking so. I had in the works a truly massive project about an altogether different subject, and the advice from virtually all sides was that I should press on with that, and leave this amusing little tale well alone.

But four people did find the story just as fascinating as I did – and saw too that by telling the poignant and human tale of William Minor, I could perhaps create some kind of prism through which to view the greater and even more fascinating story of the history of English lexicography. These four people were Bill Hamilton, my long-time friend and London agent; Anya Waddington, my editor at Viking, also in London; Larry Ashmead, the Executive Editor of HarperCollins in New York; and Marisa Milanese, then an editorial assistant in the offices of *Condé Nast Traveler* magazine, also in New York. Their faith in this otherwise unregarded project was total and unremitting, and I thank them for it unreservedly.

Marisa, who remains a paragon of ceaseless enthusiasm, dogged initiative and untiring zeal, then went on to assist me with the American end of the research; together with my close friend of a quarter-century, Juliet Walker in London, they helped me spin my basic ideas into a complex web of facts and figures, which I have since attempted to settle into some kind of coherent order. The extent to which I have succeeded or failed in this I cannot yet judge; but I should say here that these two women presented me with a bottomless well of information, and if I have misinterpreted, misread, misheard or miswritten any of it, then those mistakes are my responsibility, and mine alone.

Access to Broadmoor Special Hospital, and to the voluminous files that have been kept on all patients, was clearly going to be the key to cracking this story; and it took some weeks before Juliet Walker and I were allowed in. Paul Robertson and Alison Webster, two remarkable and kind employees of the Hospital, proved hugely helpful: without their help this book would never have managed to be much more than a collection of conjectures. The Broadmoor files provided the facts, and Paul and Alison provided the files. John Heritage and Bernard Fourness, who worked as volunteers in the Hospital Archive, gave of their own time generously, helping make some sense of the vast tonnage of paperwork.

On the other side of the Atlantic, matters proceeded rather differently – despite the best efforts of the splendid Marisa. St Elizabeth's Hospital in Washington, DC, is now no longer a federal institution, but is run by the Government of the District of Columbia – a government that has experienced some well-publicized troubles in recent years. And at first, perhaps because of this, the hospital refused point-blank to release any of its files, and went so far, quite seriously, as to suggest that I engage a lawyer and sue in order to obtain them.

However, a cursory search I made some while later of the National Archives pages on the World Wide Web suggested to me that the papers relating to Minor – who had been a patient at St Elizabeth's between 1910 and 1919, when the institution was undeniably under federal jurisdiction – might well actually be in federal custody, and not within the Kafkaesque embrace of the District. And indeed, as it turns out, they were. A couple of requests through the Internet, a happy conversation with an extremely helpful government official in College Park, Maryland, and suddenly more than 700 pages of case notes and other fascinating miscellaneous files arrived in a FedEx package. It was somewhat pleasing to be able to telephone St Elizabeth's the next day, and tell them which file I then had sitting before me on my desk. They were not best pleased.

Oxford University Press were, by contrast, wonderfully helpful; and while I am naturally happy to thank the officials at the Press who so kindly sanctioned my visits to Walton Street, I wish to acknowledge the very considerable debt that I owe first to Elizabeth Knowles, now of Oxford's Reference Books Department, who had made a study of Minor some years before and was happy to share her knowledge and access with me. I am delighted also to be able to thank the irrepressibly enthusiastic Jenny McMorris of the Press archives, who knows Minor and his remarkable legacy more intimately than anyone else, anywhere. Jenny, together with her former colleague Peter Foden, proved a tower of strength, during my visits and long after: I only hope that she manages to find an outlet for her own fascination with the great Henry Fowler, whom she rightly regards, along with Murray, as one of the true heroes of the English language.

Several friends, and a number of colleagues who had a professional interest in parts of the story, read the manuscript's early drafts, and made many suggestions for improving it. In almost all cases I have accepted their proposals with gratitude; but if on occasion I did, through carelessness or pigheadedness, disregard their warnings or demands, then the caveat about the responsibility for all errors of fact, judgement or taste remaining firmly with me applies as well: they did their best.

Among those friends I wish to thank heartily are Gully Wells, Graham Boynton, Pepper Evans, Rob Howard, Jesse Sheidlower, Nancy Stump and Paula Szuchman. And to Anthony, who complained to me that he was denied romantic favours one summer morning because his fiancée was bent on completing the reading of Chapter Nine, my apologies, and my embarrassed thanks for your forbearance.

James W. Campbell of the New Haven Historical Society gave great assistance in finding the Minor family in their old home town; the librarians and staff at the Yale Divinity Library told me much about William Minor's early life in Ceylon. Pat Higgins, an Englishwoman living in Washington state, and with whom I only corresponded by e-mail, became fascinated also by the Ceylon and Seattle ends of the Minor family story, and gave me several intriguing tips.

Michael Musick of the US National Archives then found most of Minor's military files, and Michael Rhode of the Walter Reed Army Hospital tracked down his handwritten autopsy reports. The National Park Service was helpful in giving me access to military bases in New York and Florida where he had been stationed; the Index Project in Arlington, Virginia, assisted me in finding additional records relating to his wartime career.

Susan Pakies of Virginia's Orange County tourist office, along with the immensely knowledgeable Frank Walker, then took me around all of the important sites where the Battle of the Wilderness had been fought, and later, to cheer us all up, took me to several of the delightful old inns that are hidden away in this spectacularly lovely corner of America. Jonathan O'Neal patiently explained civil war medical practice at the old Exchange Hotel-cum-hospital that is now a museum in Gordonville, Virginia.

Nancy Whitmore of the National Museum of Civil War Medicine in Frederick, Maryland, was an enthusiastic supporter of the project and painstakingly dug up a huge amount of highly relevant arcana. Dr Lawrence Kohl at the University of Alabama was kind enough to take time to discuss both the mechanics of Civil War branding, and of speculating (in an impressively informed way) of the effects such punishment might have on Irishmen who fought in the Union Army – the latter his particular speciality as an historian of the period. Mitchell Redman of New York filled in some details of Minor's later personal life, about which he had once written a short play.

Gordon Claridge of Magdalen College, Oxford, had much that was helpful to say about the origins of mental illness; Jonathan Andrews, a historian of Broadmoor, helped also; and Isa Samad of Fort Lauderdale, Florida, told me a great deal about the history of the treatment of paranoid schizophrenia.

Dale Fiore, Superintendent of the Evergreen Cemetery in New Haven, then added fascinating footnotes about the end of William Minor's life – the length of the coffin, the depth at which it is buried, the names of those who surround him in his plot.

Life became a great deal easier once I had tracked down one of the few known living relatives of William Minor, Mr Jack Minor of Riverside, Connecticut. He was kindness itself, giving me an enormous amount of useful information about the great-uncle he never knew, and offering me access to the treasure trove of pictures and papers that had sat for years, undisturbed, in a wooden box in his attic. He and his Danish wife, Birgit, became as fascinated by the story as I was, and I thank them for pleasant waterside dinners and time spent talking about the nature of their most curious relation.

204   The Surgeon of Crowthorne

David Merritt, of the Merritt International Family History Society in Swanley, Kent, gave me valuable help in ferreting out details of where George Merrett's descendants might be: I eventually found one, a Mr Dean Blanchard in Sussex, who was equally interested in the fortunes of his distant family and shared much that was valuable with me.

I am indebted also to my American agent Peter Matson, his colleague Jennifer Hengen, and to Agnes Krup who, once enthused by the strange nature of this story, became one of its keenest supporters and kept me going, writing hard, during a long hot American summer.

I should also like to record my special thanks to Sara Marafini for her splendidly alluring design of the paperback jacket.

And finally my wife Catherine saw to it that I remained undisturbed, and offered generously the kind of serenity and sanctuary that the writing of a tale like this more than amply demands and deserves: my gratitude to her is, as always, incalculable.

Simon Winchester
Wassaic, New York

Suggestions for Further Reading

The book which first inspired me to look into this story was Jonathon Green's *Chasing the Sun: Dictionary Makers and the Dictionaries They Made* (Jonathan Cape, 1996), which devoted a page and a half to the tale, and led me, via its bibliography, to the rather more celebrated work about the making of the *OED*, *Caught in the Web of Words: J. A. H. Murray and the Oxford English Dictionary* (Oxford University Press and Yale University Press, 1977), written by the great editor's granddaughter, K. M. Elisabeth Murray. In both cases the tale of the first meeting between Murray and Minor is the well-known myth; but it was not until Elizabeth Knowles wrote a more accurate account in the quarterly journal *Dictionaries* that some of the truth of the encounter became more properly recognized. Both books will delight the enthusiast: the journal tends towards the academic, but since the disciplines of lexicography are frankly not too testing, many may profit from looking at it as well.

For those interested in the basic principles behind the making of word-books, Sidney Landau's definitive *Dictionaries: The Art and Craft of Lexicography* (Cambridge University Press, 1989) is an essential read. For those iconoclasts wishing to understand the flaws in the *OED*, John Willinsky explains much in his rather ill-tempered *Empire of Words: The Reign of the OED* (Princeton University Press, 1994), which offers a politically correct revisionist view of Murray's creation – albeit from a somewhat admiring stance. It is worth reading, even if just to make the blood boil.

Copies of Dr Johnson's *Dictionary* can usually still be found quite easily – reproductions of the large-format two-volume editions have been produced on presses in such unlikely settings as the city of Beirut, from where I recently purchased a copy for $250. It is difficult to find a good original first edition for under $15,000. But there is a witty and useful distillation, with words selected by E. L. McAdam and George Milne (paperback reissued in 1995 by Cassell).

Oxford University Press deserves a history of its own, and indeed has several: I recommend Peter Sutcliffe's *The Oxford University Press: An Informal History* (Oxford University Press, 1978), which covers the saga of the making of the *OED* very well, and with reasonable impartiality.

The American Civil War is of course very comprehensively covered. The best book relating to the fighting in which Minor played a small but, for him, crucial part is Gordon C. Rhea's *The Battle of the Wilderness* (Louisiana State University Press, 1994), which I enjoyed enormously. D. P. Conyngham's 1867 classic *The Irish Brigade and Its Campaigns* has recently been reissued (Fordham University Press, New York, 1994), with an introduction by Lawrence F. Kohl, whose help with my own book I acknowledge elsewhere. Among the many books on Civil War medicine I enjoyed: George Worthington Adams's *Doctors in Blue* (Louisiana State University Press, 1980) and *In Hospital and Camp* by Harold Elk Straubing (Stackpole Books, Pennsylvania, 1993). I also took time to read the relevant chapters in the elegant giant of a book *The American Heritage New History of the Civil War* by Bruce Catton and with an introduction by James M. Macpherson (Viking, 1996), which answers every imaginable question about the minutiae of those four years of bloody fighting.

The nature of the possible mental ailments that plagued Minor, and which may have been triggered by his experiences during the war, are comprehensively explained by Gordon Claridge in *Origins of Mental Illness: Temperament, Deviance and Disorder* (Oxford University Press, 1985). Andrew Scull's splendid *Masters of Bedlam* (Princeton University Press, 1996) offers a fascinating history of the mad-doctoring trade before the times of psychiatric enlightenment.

I looked to Roy Porter – also an expert on madness and its treatment – for his rightly acclaimed social history of the city where Minor committed his murder: *London: A Social History* (Hamish Hamilton, 1994) sets the scene admirably, and remains one of the best books on England's remarkable capital.

But the one book that above all should be read in conjunction with this small volume is one of the biggest and most impressive works of scholarship to be found – the twelve-volume first edition, the 1933 supplement, the four-volume supplements of Robert Burchfield or the fully integrated twenty-volume second edition of the *Oxford English Dictionary* itself.

It makes for an expensive and bulky set of books – which is why nowadays the CD-ROM is much preferred – but it does, most importantly of all to his fans, acknowledge formally the existence and contributions of William Chester Minor. And I find that somehow the simple discovery of his name, buried as it is among the contributors who helped to make the *OED* the great totem that it remains today, is always an intensely touching moment. While it is of course in and of itself no justification for ever needing to own the great book, the finding of the name presents perhaps the finest of examples of the kind of serendipitous moment for which the *OED* is justly famous. And few would disagree that serendipity, in dictionaries, is a most splendid thing indeed.

efresh yourself at penguin.co.uk

Visit penguin.co.uk for exclusive information and interviews with
bestselling authors, fantastic give-aways and the
inside track on all our books, from the Penguin Classics
to the latest bestsellers.

BE FIRST

first chapters, first editions, first novels

EXCLUSIVES

author chats, video interviews, biographies, special
features

EVERYONE'S A WINNER

give-aways, competitions, quizzes, ecards

READERS GROUPS

exciting features to support existing groups and
create new ones

NEWS

author events, bestsellers, awards, what's new

EBOOKS

books that click – download an ePenguin today

BROWSE AND BUY

thousands of books to investigate – search, try
and buy the perfect gift online – or treat yourself!

ABOUT US

job vacancies, advice for writers and company
history

Get Closer To Penguin . . . www.penguin.co.uk